The Action Hero Teacher

Classroom Management Made Simple

KARL C. PUPÉ

© 2019 Copyright Karl C. Pupé

All Rights Reserved.

This book or any portion thereof may not be reproduced or used in any manner whatsoever without the express written permission of the publisher except for the use of brief quotations in a book review.

Printed in the United Kingdom

First Printing, 2019

Cover design by Phan Quynh

For more details, visit the author's website at www.actionheroteacher.com

To Natalie and Isabella,

Thank you for teaching me what it means to be a man, a husband and a father.

This is for you.

Contents

Introduction 1
- Why Should You Listen To Me? 5
- Who Is This Book For? 8
- What this book is NOT 9
- How To Use This Book 13

Trust Mountain 16
- What Is Trust Mountain? 17
- What Is Authority? 22
- What Is Warmth? 26
- What is Empathy? 28
- Avoid The Extremes 31

The Social Contract 39
- The Rules vs The Social Contract 40
- What is a Social Contract? 45
- How To Set Up The Social Contract 49
- The Social Contract Template 53

The Good 57
- Give them Praise 58
- Have a Sense of Humour 63
- Cast a Vision 67
- Don't Be Boring 74
- Respect the Culture 80
- Teach Grit 85
- Tell Your Story 95

The Bad 101
- Positives, Compliants & Disrupters 102
- Be Just, Fair and Firm 111
- Set Milestones 118
- Use Your Windows Effectively 123
- Check Your Body Language 130
- Talk With Authority 137

The Ugly 144
Beware Of The Emotional Hijack 145
How Well Are You Maintaining Your Engine? 153
How To Handle a Flashpoint 160
Use LAST 166
Sanction Quickly and Restore 173
Assemble Your Team 179
Get The Carers Onside 186
Interventions and Letting Go 191

Epilogue 198
Become The Hero Of Your Own Film 199
Acknowledgements 203
Bibliography 204

Introduction

Introduction

"One child, one teacher, one book, one pen can change the world."
MALALA YOUSAFZAI

"I hate all of you."
UNKNOWN STUDENT

These quotes really sum up teaching in a nutshell. One moment you feel like you are saving the world and in the next, you feel like Wily Coyote falling to the bottom of the cliff while your cheeky students look on, laughing. Teaching can often feel like the best and worst job on Earth, usually on the same day.

Many moons ago during my teacher training, I was once told that "teaching was the world's noblest profession" and that I was "educating the future leaders of tomorrow." When I entered the classroom, those feelings wore off quickly. There were days where I felt like I was a prison warden, crèche nurse, social worker, washed-up entertainer and spiritual guide. Days when I thought I should have listened to my dear old mum and tried to be a surgeon, even though I hate blood and cutting people open isn't my idea of a good time.

But in all honesty, I believe that teaching is the best job on the planet. Seriously, I'm not kidding. You will never meet more interesting people than the students in your care. For our students, our classrooms are more than places where we write the date and answer questions on Page 37 in the Big Yellow Textbook. Sometimes it can mean more than you will ever know.

Our classrooms can be places of discovery and wonder. Places where our students can discover their own unique voices and places where they can find their passions that can change their lives forever. Sadly, for our more disadvantaged students, your classroom can be a place of escape from the terrors that wait for them outside of school or at home. A place of reckoning, where they may have a conversation with someone that could stop them walking down a dark path into drugs, death or despair. Or it can simply be a place where they can keep warm as the central heating has broken and Grandad can't afford to get it repaired.

All these things happen in your classroom; you have a front-row premium seat and a tremendous opportunity to help change your students' lives for the better. It's a hard gig, but ultimately it's worth it. In a very small way, I hope that this book puts the nobility back into our profession.

Why Action Heroes?

This is your first exercise. I want you to think of your favourite action hero or heroine in film — go on close your eyes, you're safe with me. We all have them.

If you're anything like me, you may have thought of:

- The ice-cold glare of Clint Eastwood in *Pale Rider*
- The power walk of Denzel Washington in *Man On Fire*
- The fiery determination of Sigourney Weaver in *Aliens*
- The breathtaking bravery of Jackie Chan in *Police Story*
- The graceful strength of Gal Gadot in *Wonder Woman*

Although we cannot fight monstrous aliens, take down mafia cartels with a quip and a smile, or move faster than a speeding bullet, we love these heroes because they often have qualities that we wish that we could embody. Our heroes can be cool, calm and calculated in the face of trouble. When the chips are down, and things look bad, our heroes often come up with a brilliant plan that helps them to save the day and look good while doing it. Our heroes take action, they are never passive and they always seem to do the right thing even when it hurts.

Now I want you to imagine you were like that in your classroom.

But we don't often feel like that, do we?

Now I want you to imagine the toughest class that you have to teach regularly. Nod your head if, before you took the class, you felt:

- Afraid?
- Anxious?

INTRODUCTION

- Full of dread?
- Depressed?
- Fed up?

Yep, this has included me too and trust me — this is not good for you nor your students. But I'm here to tell you that it's OK to feel like that because even our greatest heroes go through some tight spots.

However, by the time the credits are rolling, they have won and you can too. My sincere hope is that this book will act as the Yoda to your Luke Skywalker: giving you the tools, the wisdom and the power to walk into your classroom and despite your fear, take that class by storm.

Welcome aboard Captain, it's time to set sail.

Why Should You Listen To Me?

I know what you're thinking… "OK 'tough guy,' why should I listen to you?" Good question — my mother taught me not to talk to strangers too. I've been in the Education sector for eight years, and I have been very fortunate to have worked in some great roles including:

- Working as a one-to-one teacher's assistant with children with severe Special Educational Needs (SEN) and Social, Emotional and Mental Health needs (SEMH) both in primary and secondary schools.
- Being a NEETs coordinator. I ran projects aimed at 16 - 19 year olds in East London that were **N**ot in **E**ducation, **E**mployment or **T**raining and were at high risk of committing or becoming victims of anti-social behaviour. These behaviours included gang violence, robbery, assault, drug dealing and usage. Believe it or not, this only took up half my time. The other half was taken up by organising and running classes for students who had been kicked out of mainstream education in Years 8 through 11. These students were at risk of becoming NEETs, so they needed "high touch" interventions designed to keep them engaged in their lessons.
- I was a secondary school supply teacher in inner-city London… Some days it was like *Downturn Abbey*, some days it was like *Dangerous Minds*…
- Helped to run the Behaviour Management Department in a mixed state secondary school that dealt with students who were too disruptive to stay in class and were in danger of being permanently excluded.
- Being a fully qualified teacher - so I have all those fancy letters after my name that say that I can teach people.
- I have received a Diploma in Leadership and Management. This piece of paper says that I have the skills to coach, lead and troubleshoot as an 'executive manager.' It's fancier than

INTRODUCTION

it sounds.

But outside of Education, I had many high pressure jobs that forced me to deal with some really tough characters.

- I was a telephone double glazing salesman - I used to cold call people in the middle of their dinners and try to sell them guttering, fascias and soffits - I still don't know what those things are. Usually, I was greeted with "How did you get my number?" Or "Is this a prank?" This was before I was sworn at like a man who asked out their Grandma on a hot date.
- I was a telecoms account manager - I worked for a large telecommunications company which was great at taking your money but not giving you any service. I looked after 100 medium to large scale businesses, and I was their designated first point of contact for all their telephony needs. In all honesty, all I got was their problems, usually involving broken telephone lines which stopped their enterprise making money. When they called in, I was often met with swear words. Most of the conversations were somewhere between Hulk levels of rage and childlike pleading about getting their services fixed. I had a customer breakdown in tears saying that if we didn't fix his line in an hour, that his business would go under and I would make him and his family homeless. This job didn't make me feel warm and fuzzy on the inside.
- I was a high-end furniture salesman - I worked for a major department store in London's West End that catered to the upper echelons of society. People who are wealthy weren't always the kindest customers, especially to a 'commoner.' I met Former Home Secretary Jack Straw and one of the guys (I can't remember his name) from the pop band Hear'Say - good times.
- I was a street promotions staff member - I used to stand in the middle of a busy train station or high street, trying to offer you things from brands that you didn't know, want or need. Usually, it was some form of leaflets or trying to get

you to give us your email so that we can harass you digitally. Through rain, sleet, snow and sunshine, I stood in the street being rejected and sworn at.

- I was a battle rapper - 100% true and many decades ago. Think *8 Mile* but with less talent and no money. Again, I was being sworn at and insulted about everything from my clothes to my background. Many of the battle rappers seemed to obsess about my mum as they always used to talk about her and tell me what they wanted to do to her. In the space of a minute, I had to think of something smart and witty to defeat my opponent, but I often spoke about their parents too. If you went too far, you may win the battle but could find yourself taking a free ride courtesy of the London Ambulance Service to the hospital. These were often high pressure situations.

- Host of an urban talent event in Central London. Usually, if the crowd did not like the act or if something went wrong, they were not afraid to let out their 'feelings' often using swear words. You wouldn't think it, but hosts often took the blame for things that were outside of their control, like lighting, guest-lists and payment of the performers. Between dealing with acts who thought that they were famous (but never shifted one record), to dealing with angry guests, thieving managers and lazy staff, I found myself between a rock and a hard place on a weekly basis.

Guess what? Each of those jobs required me to deal with people who were angry, nasty, confrontational and aggressive. For the record, I got more abuse from any one of those jobs than all my years of teaching put together. But through training and hard-earned experience, I received some fantastic instruction on how to handle difficult individuals, which I will now share with you.

INTRODUCTION

Who Is This Book For?

I wrote this book for:

- People who are considering taking a PGCE/EAT/Initial Teacher Training Qualification and don't feel prepared to take on the classroom
- The Newly Qualified Teacher (NQT) who has excellent subject knowledge but feels overwhelmed by classroom management
- The teacher who may have a set of tough classes where behaviour is a massive challenge
- The teacher who cannot engage with their students and cannot understand why
- Teachers who teach students that have Social Emotional and Mental Health needs (SEMH).

I wrote this book for teachers that have to deal with teenagers (eleven through to nineteen). If you teach in secondary schools and further education colleges, then this is for you.

If you teach younger learners then don't be deterred. Having taught in the Primary education (KS1 & KS2), much of the material can be mapped to your classrooms. Use the parts that apply and discard the rest.

That also goes for teachers outside of 'traditional education.' Youth workers, mentors and supporters may find some new approaches that they can try with their mentees. If you have any questions, I would love to hear from you. I will leave my contact details at the end of the book.

What this book is NOT

Please read this before you buy the book. Seriously.

If you are anything like me, before I buy a book, I like to skim-read the pages; either physically in the bookshop or previewing it on an eCommerce store like Amazon. This is why I have put this page at the beginning, just so that you know what type of party you're entering. My 'old man' once preached to me that the foundation of any great relationship is TRUTH and RESPECT and without those two things, your relationship is doomed. Dear reader, because I respect your intelligence and your money, I want to tell you the TRUTH and lay it all out on the table before we go further.

If, from reading the following group of statements, you don't like the direction that this book is going in, by all means, put the book down or turn off the previewer and thank you again for giving my book a skim. The last thing I would want you to do is to be misled. I don't want any 'one-star' reviews on Amazon if I can help it. I genuinely wish to help you guys, but I realise this may not be for everyone — it's your call.

This book is NOT a Theory book. This is a Practice book.

I've eaten my own dog food here. Everything that I am telling you, I have either done or continue to do now. For my own quality assurance purposes, I have spoken to many working teachers of all backgrounds and compared notes to make sure that I don't sound like a madman. These theories and practices have been tried and tested in the fires of frontline teaching and have been my go-to solutions for my peers and me for many years.

Yes, I have drawn from many different academic theories and practices over my teaching career, and where I have, I will happily reference them. But the majority of these techniques were borne out of many trials, experiments and deep reflections. If you have come here looking for the "similarities and differences between Freudian and Jungian philosophies on Teaching Pedagogy" you're in the wrong place, Charlie. Besides, when a student is threatening to throw a chair at me, I never once went to grab an academic paper for protection.

This book is NOT complex.

You got me. Much of what I have written has been said before by a variety of different people over the years. I have read many books and gone to training seminars that focused on psychology, emotional intelligence, leadership, philosophy and yes, teaching pedagogy. If you read enough of these books, they all start saying the same things and much of it is common sense. But why am I going to all this trouble to write this book for? Because as my wise uncle used to say, "Common sense is not always common practice."

For example, we know that if we save some of our wages and invest them in high-interest savings accounts, in a couple of decades, we will have a significant amount of loot. We know that if we want to stay slim and healthy, we need to cut out the junk food and carbs, eat more greens and do some regular exercise that gets our blood pumping. Yet we still have hundreds, possibly thousands of books being written about finance and healthy living every year. Everyone is different. My aim is not to give you a bunch of theories that would look great in an essay, but a bunch of tools and processes that will help you RIGHT NOW. This book is about giving you different options. Tweak it to your style of teaching.

I've deliberately tried to keep this book simple for a reason. I'm sure, like me, you have read books where it sounded like the author was a living dictionary. They have made it their life mission to put as many fancy, complicated words on one page as possible. Those books often serve as excellent sleep aids and that's not what I want to do here, readers. I like to keep things conversational and breezy — it will keep you awake and hopefully, it will help you in the classroom.

This book is NOT a "positive thinking" book.

These types of books get a bad rap and to be honest, I totally understand why. There are some great self-help books out there that genuinely set out to help their readers. But there is the other type — you know what I'm talking about. The one that makes you scream affirmations of "I AM WONDERFUL" in the mirror fifty times, the one that talks about having a "positive mindset" 24 hours a day, 365 days of the year. But that is not reality. Johnny Tableflipper will let you know how wonderful you are, quickly.

As much as teaching can be a satisfying career, it can be complicated. Life happens to our students (and us), and it's about accepting reality and dealing with it. "Positive thinking" really does help but only if it's matched with "positive action."

I won't be asking you to do the impossible either. I know that you have a massive amount on your plate already so asking you to meditate for two hours a day will not cut it. As you will see later, I designed this book with this in mind. Do a little and do it often and you will see the path.

This book is NOT a Quick-Fix. The book will only work if you do.

I'm sure like me you have seen books with titles like:

"Learn Web Design in One Hour"

"Become a Property Millionaire in 30 Days"

"Get a Movie Star Body in One Week"

"Learn Brain Surgery Over A Weekend or Your Money Back!"

This is not that book. Besides, if people could do all those things in a week, why do we have university courses in those subjects? Have I missed a trick here? Jokes aside, the subtitle of this book is "Classroom Management Made SIMPLE" not INSTANT. To master any craft, whether it's chess, entrepreneurship or football,

11

INTRODUCTION

takes years of practice, study and constructive feedback. Although most of my suggestions are simple, in many cases, I am asking you to implement behaviours that may not be familiar to you, and it will take TIME before you can see any results. Also, every class is different so you may have to make tiny tweaks for it suit your style, so please experiment.

My advice is to work with this book for at least three months and track your progress. My aim for you is simple: I want you to improve by 1% every day. That's almost nothing, right? But imagine this: If at the beginning of the year, you taught from Monday to Friday every day and we took out all the weekends, holidays and special events, we would be left with roughly 250 working days. If you improved by 1% every day, you would be TWO AND A HALF TIMES better at the end of the year than you were at the beginning. That's the plan.

Well, that's my disclaimers done. If you're happy to continue then let's go deeper underground.

How To Use This Book

Here's a brief overview of what each section does.
Before We Set Off, Pack Your Kit

A colleague of mine is an avid camper and often took our students on camping expeditions on behalf of our school.

As well as teaching our students how to light a fire, cook and read a map, he always made sure that they had their survival kit. The special pack contained the key items like a First Aid kit, water filters, a compass and a map — the essentials that would keep them alive and get them home. This kit gave the students (and the teachers) confidence that they could manage the trip ahead, whatever obstacles came their way.

In the next two chapters, I will give you a Classroom Management Survival Kit to help you manage the behaviour in your classroom. The "Trust Mountain" and "Social Contract" chapters are the theory elements that I have built all my classroom management strategies on. These are my guiding principles that I always return to in my difficult days and my darkest nights.

I could give you all the tips and tricks in the world, but if you do not know WHY you are using these tactics and WHAT the result should be, then it's pointless. It's like me telling you to get in your car, buy a full tank of petrol and bomb it down the motorway — without giving you a place to go.

When I started my work with my SEMH students, I used every tip, trick and gimmick I could to try and engage them... And they handed me back my backside every time. Luckily, I had fantastic mentors who helped me back on my feet, patched me up and set me loose in the classroom with upgraded knowledge and skills. Like my camping colleague, I'm telling you that if you don't take this toolkit onboard, you won't get the rest of this book.

After you have mastered those chapters, the next three parts will contain the individual strategies that you can action in your classroom. The sections are:

The Good

These are what I call "positive behaviour strategies" or to put it more simply, strategies that make you and the learner feel good when you use them. These strategies can be used to encourage, motivate and positively challenge your students. These tips help you to understand your learners, build rapport, find their strengths and weaknesses and hopefully let everyone have some fun.

But as we know, life is not that simple...

The Bad

These strategies are for low-level disruption or, in other words, behaviour that slows down the lesson, irritates others and generally makes our job harder. If you have ever felt that you struggled to get through a session because of calling out, messing around and chatting constantly, then these tips are for you.

The Ugly

These are the interruptions that teachers dread. This section is to deal with what I call "severe disruptions and incidents." In a nutshell, this is where the whole lesson has to stop to deal with the crisis at hand. This may involve aggression towards you or other students or where the student is utterly disengaged and will not positively respond to anything that you have to say. This can be really tough to wrestle with, but these strategies will help you deal with it in the classroom head on.

It is said that "prevention is better than the cure" - I agree. In this section, I will give you the tools that can help you work behind the scenes with your most challenging learners and help you create trust, resolve problems and install boundaries to help you prevent major episodes occurring in your class. No matter what institution you are in, one day you will find yourself facing an "ugly" situation. Hopefully, you will now have the tools to face it.

It's a Buffet, Not a Three Course Meal

I designed this text to be a workbook, not a coffee table decoration. If you have the paperback version, you have my complete permission to use and abuse this book. Write in the margins, take notes, answer the questions and keep coming back again and again until you have those particular techniques mastered. Those with the Kindle version can do the same but electronically. The more you put in, the more you get out.

Of course, you can read the book from cover to cover, but I want you to be a little more intentional than that. So, here's what I suggest.

STEP 1: Read both the "Trust Mountain" and "Social Contract" sections and tattoo in your mind all the key points that are in these chapters. This is mandatory reading. Keep referring back to it if necessary.

STEP 2: Read "The Good," The Bad," and "The Ugly" sections and highlight any tips and tricks that you really want to try.

STEP 3: Once you have reached the end of the book, go back and select one "good," one "bad" and one "ugly" strategy that you would like to try with your classes. Read the Reflection Questions then WRITE DOWN THE ANSWERS. These questions are designed so that you can reflect and see precisely where you are. I can't do it for you.

STEP 4: Once you have reflected, try them out in your classroom. Do this over at least a week and then reflect on what went RIGHT or what went WRONG. If it worked, congratulations, keep on going! If it did not work for your learners then that's OK, find another tip and apply that. Once you have mastered the three skills that you chose, then go back to Step 2. Rinse and repeat.

Remember the techniques that you are going to learn could be going against years or even decades of students' behaviour patterns, and you may find some resistance. Don't lose heart — think small steps, not huge bounds.

You're ready. It's time to climb the mountain.

Trust Mountain

What Is Trust Mountain?

Grand Teton National Park Mountains, Wyoming[1]

Look at those mountains. Beautiful, aren't they? Well, like Indiana Jones, Lara Croft or Sir Ranulph Fiennes, you are taking your learners on a journey up a mountain similar to this one. This journey can be one that is filled with wonder and adventure for you and your apprentices. But on the other hand, if you don't respect the mountain, you will find yourself falling faster than the British Pound after the 2016 Brexit Referendum.

When it comes to classroom management, a mental model that has served me very well over the years is what I called the 'Trust Mountain.' It's quite simple:

The more your students respect you and the more you can build a healthy working relationship with them, the more they will enjoy their lessons and behave positively.

This is achieved by using two things:

1. Authority - Your students respect you as their teacher and respond well to your instructions and guidance.
2. Warmth - In this book, 'warmth' is described as the ability to

empathise with your students and understand their needs. This includes understanding your own emotions, motivations and personality and how they synergise with your learners.

This mental model was much inspired by the acclaimed psychologist Abraham Maslow and his famous "Hierarchy Of Needs."

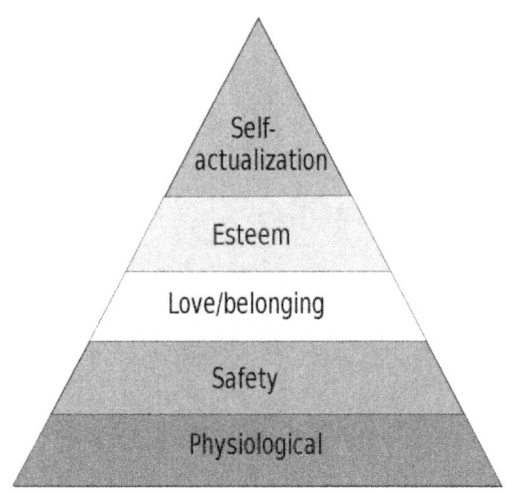

Maslow's Hierarchy Of Needs[2]

Abraham Maslow, in his 1943 paper "A Theory Of Human Motivation", stated that human beings have five levels of needs which are ranked by importance: the basic ones like physical safety and security being at the bottom with the more personal and life-affirming ones like purpose and self-esteem being at the top. Maslow wrote:

> "Human needs arrange themselves in hierarchies of pre-potency. That is to say, the appearance of one need usually rests on the prior satisfaction of another, more-potent need[3]."

In other words, if you don't satisfy the basic needs such as physical safety and shelter, then you can't advance to the higher stages like purpose and relationships. If you put me in a locked room with an angry Siberian tiger, I can 100% guarantee you that I will not be thinking about whether I am "self-actualised."

You must understand that your students' behaviour and needs are very closely related. If you don't understand them, then you can't influence them. Over the years, I started to form my own theory to help me teach my NEET students, and that became Trust Mountain.

Similar to Maslow's Hierarchy, we aim to take our students as high up the mountain as possible. Let's do a quick tour of what to expect starting from the lowest level.

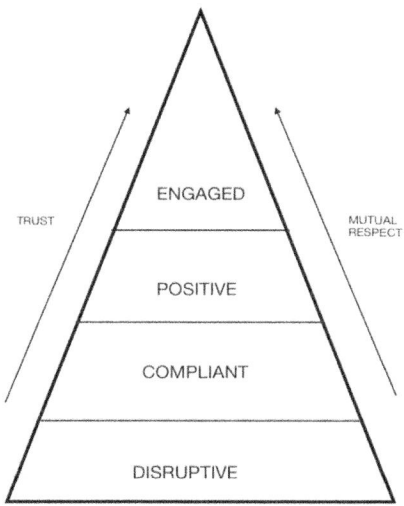

1. Disruptive

The Red Zone. The Dark Night of the Soul. The Hurt Locker. This is the area we all hate and make the lives of everyone in the classroom a living hell. These students don't respect you, they will not respond to you in any positive way and they are openly hostile to you. You don't enjoy teaching them either, so it becomes a vicious cycle.

The classroom feels negative and, everyone is counting the

minutes until the lesson is over. There is no relationship between the student and the teacher. This is where Johnny Tableflipper and Meagan Rubberthrower live. Disruptive students can age you five years in one hour - and your anti-ageing cream can't save you.

These students severely disrupt the class and there seems to be absolutely nothing that you can do about it. The room is lawless and they know it, pushing you to your absolute limits. You spend much of your lesson either shouting, calling for help or asking yourself "Why did I become a teacher?" This is where many of "Ugly" tips, tricks and strategies come into play.

2. Compliant

The Yellow Zone. This level is slightly better as they will listen to you and follow your instructions, but they will do the absolute minimum. The Compliant level is usually the home of "low-level disruption" where students who are not fully engaged will talk, make noise and generally annoy other people. Students at this level tend to be more afraid of being punished, but their antics will slow your lesson down.

The constant nagging, negotiating and interruptions can be very draining and not the world-changing, difference-making job you were promised during your teacher training. Although you still may have to challenge poor behaviour, you can at this level start to get a greater understanding of your students and there's a little more give and take. This is where the "Bad" strategies will come in handy and help you build your authority and trust with your pupils.

3. Positive

The Green Zone. You're making headway. Students in this zone respect you and start to engage with you and join in the learning. Students who are in the Positive zone respect your judgement, and get on with the tasks with minimum fuss.

At this level, students can review their behaviour and self-correct when needed. They have become more reflective and they can see how their actions affect everyone around them. Because you have a rapport with your students, you can now start to tailor specific lessons or tasks to take advantage of the favourable environment. The sessions run more smoothly, and everyone's happier to be in the room.

4. Engaged

The Blue Zone. As the great philosopher Aubrey "Drake" Graham said, "we started from the bottom, and now we here." These are the lessons that you see on the "Get Into Teaching" adverts. At this level, students buy into you as their teacher. Your pupils are motivated to learn, take full responsibility for their learning, and you find that disruptive behaviour has virtually disappeared out of the classroom. You feel relaxed and enjoy teaching your classes. This is the good stuff.

But I don't want to sell you a pipe dream. Like you, your students are humans. This is a very fluid idea. Students are not fixed across the board and change as fast as the British weather. Some students can be disruptive in one subject and be fully engaged in another. I have regularly seen students go from being absolute terrors to lovely little cherubs because they had a different teacher covering their lesson. This could be daunting, especially if you have classes full of Disrupters. Your ultimate goal would be to get all your students to become Engaged and have every cohort behave absolutely perfect. But that's a dream. That could take years for you to do with every single group that you teach. Although it is not impossible, I want to think about today.

If your class looks like the World War II Normandy Beach invasion scene in Saving Private Ryan, all I want you to do is ask yourself this simple question:

"No matter where they are at on Trust Mountain, how can I get most of my students to go up ONE level?"

To do that, we will need to look at AUTHORITY and why this so crucial in your classroom.

What Is Authority?

The word "authority" has been given a bad rap nowadays. Images of power-hungry dictators and Machiavellian CEOs flash on our news screens every single day.

'Authority' has become the naughty nickname of 'power,' and now receives the same distrust and fear. In our time, societies around the world have become more sensitive to people and institutions that abuse their power. More than ever, people are prepared to question, critique and challenge the powers that be and hold them to account — which of course is the right thing to do.

But before we kick 'authority' out of the home, change the house keys and talk to our lawyers, let's take a closer look at what the word actually means and see if we can give it a fair trial. The Oxford Dictionary has several definitions of the word.[4]

> 1. [mass noun] The power or right to give orders, make decisions, and enforce obedience.
>
> 'he had absolute authority over his subordinates'
>
> 'a rebellion against those in authority.'

Yikes. This is the 'scary' authority that we were talking about. But there's more…

> 3. [mass noun] The power to influence others, especially because of one's commanding manner or one's recognised knowledge about something.
>
> 'he has the natural authority of one who is used to being obeyed'
>
> 3.1 The confidence resulting from personal expertise.
>
> 'he hit the ball with authority'
>
> 3.2 [count noun] A person with extensive or specialised knowledge about a subject; an expert.
>
> 'he was an authority on the stock market.'

'Authority' is so much more than barking orders and making people cower before you. Your authority can include your expertise, your experiences, wisdom and your ability to pass on your knowledge to your students. These are things not to be sniffed at.

If you want further proof about the power of positive authority, I want you to imagine you are on your way to work and you see a stranger lying in the road, unconscious and in bad condition. You freeze — apart from the basic First Aid training you learnt at the Cadets, you don't know how you can help this person.

All of a sudden, a woman quickly runs up to you and tells you that she's a doctor. She checks the patient at lightning speed and reassures him that help is on the way. She instructs you to help her put him in the recovery position, meanwhile giving clear instructions to the gathered passers-by to call the ambulance and grab a jacket to keep the injured man warm. When the ambulance does arrive, she perfectly relays to the paramedics what is wrong with him and what he may need at the hospital, calmly and efficiently.

The doctor was calm, assertive and entirely in control of the situation. Although all hell was breaking loose, she kept it together and got this group of strangers that had never met before to work in unison to help this injured man. She went beyond having authority — she became a leader.

Many men and women a lot smarter than me have discussed this very subject for centuries and come up with libraries of academic papers on the subject. But for our text, I just want to talk about two flavours: Positional Authority and Personal Authority.

Positional Authority

This is also known as 'Institutional Authority.' This is the authority that is gained by having a particular position, title or social standing. Positional Authority is very closely related to power, which is the ability to make people do what you want, whether they like it or not. In our society, the more positional power you have, the more money, connections and fame you receive. This type of authority is external — other people can see it and in some cases, must obey it. For example, The Prime Minister has more Positional Authority in the whole of the United Kingdom than the Mayor of London.

Authority doesn't just exist in politics, but anywhere where there is an organisation of people. Wherever you get a group of people acting together, there will always be a leader and others that must follow.

As a teacher in charge of students, you are naturally in a position of authority. You are responsible for their wellbeing and safety, and you are the 'top dog' in your class. But Positional Authority is not enough by itself to be able to lead people over the long term.

With the internet, our tech-savvy students have been given a platform to express themselves and voice their opinions more than any other youths in human history and they expect to be heard — whether we, the adults, agree or not.

If you only use Positional Authority to 'get your way,' the most you will ever get is compliance. Your students will do as you ask, but they will drag their heels and use guerrilla tactics to disrupt your lesson. But that's not the end of the story.

Personal Authority

Personal Authority is an entirely different beast altogether. This authority comes from who you are as a person, rather than the title that you hold. Leadership expert Robert C. Maxwell has described this trait as 'influence'. In his book "The 21 Irrefutable Laws of Leadership" Maxwell lists the traits that make up influence as:

"Character - who you are

Relationships - who you know

Knowledge - what you know

Intuition - what you feel

Experience - where you have been

Past success — what you've done

Ability - what you can do[5]."

Personal Authority includes how you treat others, how you 'show-up' in relationships, your own values and your boundaries — what lines that you would not cross with others and don't expect others to cross with you. Your Personal Authority also includes your competence, your ability to solve problems, your reliability and how you are under pressure.

Sometimes a person's Personal Authority is so great that it can overshadow people who have greater Positional Authority.

When I was an account manager, I worked with a wonderful man named Vince who had been with the company for many years. Although Vince and I shared the same job title, Vince's incredible expertise around telecommunications and his company-wide contacts made him absolutely invaluable to our team. An unwritten rule in our department was "If you have a big problem — ask Vince." His troubleshooting skills were legendary, and even the General Manager would consult Vince from time to time. His Personal Authority was unrivalled.

Positional Authority may get you to the front of the house, but it's Personal Authority that unlocks the door. If you are a teacher, lecturer or mentor you already have Positional Authority. Building your Personal Authority comes with time, patience and self-development. But if you continue to work on it, you can transform your classroom.

So, remember this equation:

AUTHORITY = Position (your role) + Influence (who you are, what you do and how you do it).

What Is Warmth?

Like "authority" the word "warmth" has also been warped. Images of the kiddie's tea-parties *Mary Poppins* and *Barney the Purple Dinosaur* probably come to mind. But far from being a weakness, when combined with authority, can be a formidable strength.

In her book, *The Charisma Myth*, Olivia Fox Cabane argues that great leaders like Nelson Mandela and Princess Diana had another quality as well as power, which is "warmth." Fox stated "Warmth, simply put, is goodwill towards others…Being seen as warm means being perceived as any of the following: benevolent, altruistic, caring, or willing to impact our world in a positive way[6]"

The cynics amongst you might think "I'm not running a country, I'm dealing with a bunch of misbehaving students!" OK, fine. I'll bite. I want you to think about the best teacher that you ever had. What qualities did they have? Were they kind? Were they patient? Did they "get" you? I have asked this question many times over the years and I have always received the same answers. The teachers that we remember are not only the ones that taught us about a particular subject, but also cared and encouraged us to be the very best that we can be.

John C. Maxwell wrote this about good leaders: "When leaders show respect for others — especially for people who have less power or a lower position than theirs — they gain respect from others[7]." Teachers that are warm and maintain their self-respect inspire people to follow them.

Two aspects help us achieve "warmth": emotional intelligence and empathy.

What Is Emotional Intelligence?

Our society calls smart people "geniuses" and "masterminds." But how would we describe individuals who are good at handling emotions?

Daniel Goleman, science journalist and bestselling author, would describe these people as 'emotionally intelligent'. Goleman wrote that emotional intelligence allows the individual to control their "impulse[s] and delay gratification, to regulate one's moods and to keep distress from swamping the ability to think; to empathise and to hope[8]."

Emotional intelligence is your ability to take stock of the situation at hand, understand how it affects you and your students, and choose the correct response. As an educator, you must have a good understanding of what makes you, the teacher, 'tick' in the classroom. You must recognise the things that make you happy, sad, angry or irritated when you stand in front of your classes.

When you're a teacher, there is nowhere to hide. Your students are always watching you and will follow your example in how you handle your emotions. Your emotional intelligence is a big factor in how your students look at you and whether they will accept your leadership. If we do not have a handle on ourselves, then we won't be able to have a handle on our learners. Know yourself, then know your students.

What is Empathy?

The Cambridge Dictionary describes empathy as "the ability to share someone else's feelings or experiences by imagining what it would be like to be in that person's situation[9]."

Young lives matter. We don't teach robots but growing human beings. It is easy to forget but beyond our classrooms; our students have incredibly rich inner and outer lives.

If you teach secondary and further education level students, you must realise that our young charges are on the doorstep to adulthood, which for them is both exciting but incredibly frightening too.

Their bodies are changing at an incredible rate and so are their emotions and consciousnesses. As alien as it may be now, we must remember what it was like for us when we went through that stage and, as adults, gently guide them to become successful, healthy and mature human beings. Your students will stumble, they will fall, but as educators, it is our job to teach them how to get up and keep going forward. Our ability to have empathy is proportional to our ability to lead.

The Student Triangle

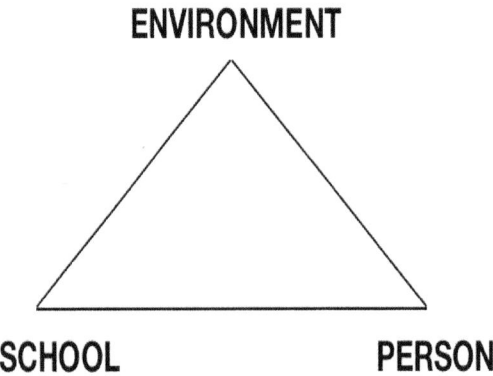

Teachers can sometimes think that we are the 'Centres of The Universe.' When you have a student, who seems like they have been sent by Tom Cruise of the Impossible Missions Force to upset you and disrupt your lessons, it can feel that everything is your fault. But our students, like ourselves, are complex beings and we are only seeing one side of a multi-faceted diamond. Another mentor of mine gave me this mental model called the "Student Triangle" which helped me understand and empathise with my students, and I am offering it to you.

There are lots of factors which can determine how your students 'turn up' in your classroom, but they fall broadly into three main areas: 'The Person,' 'The Environment' and 'The School.' Let's break it down a little more:

The Person

- Their personality traits — curious, laidback, restless
- Their temperaments — do they tend to be happy, sad, irritable,
- Their likes/dislikes — what are their favourite subjects? Who are their main role models?
- Their academic abilities — where do their natural talents lie? Are they scientists, artists or sportspeople?
- Whether they have learning difficulties — do they have Special Educational Needs (SEN) or Social Emotional Mental Health needs (SEMH)? If they do, is the institution providing adequate care for these students?

Their Environment

- Their family life — how many siblings do they have? Who are their primary caregivers?
- Their culture — this can be anything from their ethnic, religious or national identity
- Their friendship groupings in your class — does their behaviour change when they are around certain people?
- Their location — what is the town like where they live? Is it a suburb? The inner city? Do they come from outside the

area?
- What are their aspirations? Will they go to college? University? Learn a trade? Take up an apprenticeship?

Their School Life

- Their previous school/college experience — primary, secondary etc.
- How long have they been in the school — have they been in the school the whole way through or have they just arrived?
- Their relationship with you — do they get on with you? What are their relationships like with other teachers?
- Their relationships with authority — do they dislike being told what to do? Are their particular tones or words that rile them up?
- Their perspective of the school — do they feel that they can get support that they need? Can they talk to someone about their school/college life? Do they feel that the adults in the institution listen to them and take on their concerns?

I am sure that there are plenty of questions that you could add to my list, and this is not exhaustive. The bottom line is that these three areas have a significant influence on how your student engages in your classroom and the more details that you know, within appropriate professional boundaries, will help you to build a positive relationship that will take you further up Trust Mountain.

So, remember this equation:

WARMTH = Emotional Intelligence (Understanding your own emotions and responding correctly) + Empathy (Understanding your students' needs and knowing how to serve them)

Avoid The Extremes

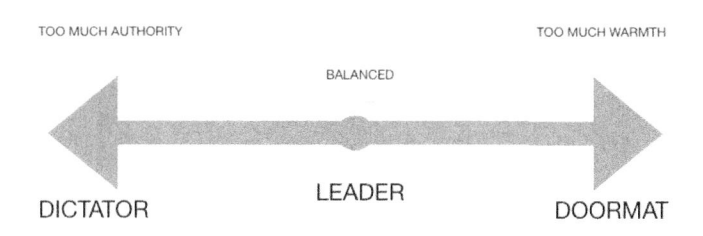

```
TOO MUCH AUTHORITY              TOO MUCH WARMTH
              BALANCED
    ←—————————————————————→
     DICTATOR    LEADER    DOORMAT
```

All of us have a classroom management style naturally. If there is a Classroom Management Spectrum, with extreme authority on the far left and extreme warmth on the far right, we will all fall somewhere in between.

The age group and the type of students that you teach will have a significant impact on your style. For example, when I was a teaching assistant in a primary school, I was once tasked with looking after the Year 1 students. Their behaviour wasn't really an issue, but they needed a lot more tenderness and attention. The Year 1 children were delightful – apart from when they were vomiting, soiling themselves, sneezing without covering their mouth and many other unpleasant things. Whereas when I taught in secondary schools, I needed to be firmer and stand my ground a lot more — especially when I was called a "wasteman" several times.

As a rule of thumb, great teachers seem to have a good mix of both: they are kind, empathetic, caring and yet have the respect of their students and can correct and challenge them when needed. They are masters knowing when to say the right things, to the right student at the right time. They facilitate dynamic, productive classrooms that everyone can enjoy. They have the Positional Authority but have also built up a lot of Personal Authority not only with their students but with the broader learning community.

BALANCED

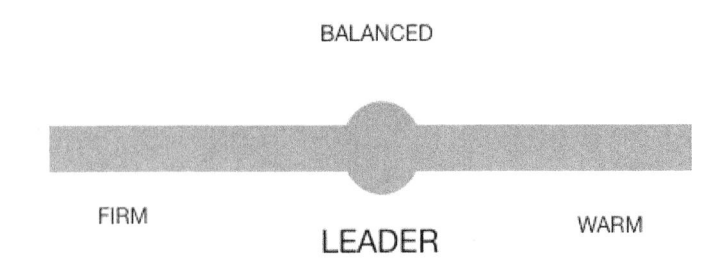

FIRM　　　　　WARM

LEADER

There are times that you may find yourself slightly 'off-centre' — where you may be leaning on your authority a bit more (left-of-centre) or building working relationships with your challenging students (right-of-centre), but that's perfectly fine. Different students, classes, institutions and years will require separate approaches. Give yourself some flexibility.

However, I must give you a severe warning. From my teaching experience and witnessing other people's teaching practice, it is never a good idea to go to either extreme. Using three examples, let's look at Mike the Dictator, Toby the Doormat and Mr Patrick the Yo-Yo.

The Dictator

All Authority, No Warmth

Mike's favourite films were war films. He loved the guts, the glory and winning at all costs. He would often imagine himself as the general, giving orders and expecting the soldiers to follow them without question — and this exactly how he taught. Mike started his new secondary school, and he knew that he had to hit the ground running. Mike ignored any students who greeted him and would beckon them inside when he was ready to teach. He expected them to enter the class in silence and if they didn't, he would make them all go outside and start again. "Don't smile until December," Mike would say to his colleagues in the Staffroom and he was determined to keep his promise.

Mike always gave the same threats and revelled in the fear that his warnings created. If his students broke any of his 500 rules, they would earn a sanction, and he would scream with furious anger at those who questioned his judgement. The well-behaved students feared him while the more challenging students resented his regime. But he got the results, and to Mike, that's all that mattered — after all, they come to school to pass their GCSEs not have fun.

But after a while, things started to turn for the worst. Mike's students became demotivated, as they were terrified to ask a question, let alone talk to him about how their learning was going. Whenever a student did show him their work, he would always point out the errors, destroying their confidence and enthusiasm. Mike noticed that the class' academic performance dipped as the months went on, but he put it down to 'laziness and entitlement' and wasn't curious why.

Then Oscar came. Oscar in 10B, the school's Bad-Boy-In-Chief, was transferred to Mike's class and they instantly hated each other. Mike thought that screaming instructions at him would do the trick and Oscar argued back. During one of their exchanges, Oscar snapped and told Mike that he was a "crap teacher" and that "he ran his class like a prison." Mike turned purple: turning up the volume in an already heated battle. Oscar was taken out of the class and given an afterschool sanction. It was on: Oscar vowed to make life as difficult for Mike as possible and that was the start of the "Science War."

Oscar and a couple of his friends started truanting, doing everything to avoid his lessons and if they did come in, then the barrage of insults and abuse came raining in the classroom like mortar fire. Some of the better-behaved students went to the Head of Science requesting to switch sets and the teaching assistants, technicians and everybody else hated going there. Mike loved wars and now he found himself in a daily one.

The Doormat

All Warmth, No Authority

When Toby was younger, he hated it when the teachers shouted at him and as he filled his PGCE application, Toby vowed to do better. During his teacher training, Toby thought that he would never need to shout as he was going to be "the teacher that he never had in school." He was going to be hip, cool and "down with the kids." Toby started his first teaching job in a local inner city college that had been known for having students with challenging behaviour. "No pressure," Toby said to himself as he walked into his first class. Toby insisted that they called him by his first name, as he wanted to show 'he was on their side.'

At first, the class ran smoothly. Toby was a massive Chelsea fan so, he spent much of his time talking about football with the challenging students as they chuckled and joked together. But as time went on less and less work was being done, with the students playing on their phones and not bringing their books in. Toby, fearful that he would destroy what he worked so hard to gain, would let them off their classwork while they chilled in the classroom.

The well-behaved students became frustrated: Toby seemed to reward the challenging students for their bad behaviour, so why should they work hard? The challenging students seemed not to bother with their homework and the standards started to slip. Gradually the students stopped laughing with Toby and started laughing *at* him, making jokes at his expense. Toby thought that this was 'banter' and that they would "come around soon." The stronger personalities in the class started to 'hold court', walking around, shouting and disrupting the classroom despite Toby's protests. Toby began to feel that he was losing his authority.

One of his mentors observed his classes and saw the lack of work being done and highlighted this to Toby. Toby had to do something. He decided that the following week that there would be a new regime, no more playing games. Toby started demanding silence in his lessons and tried to crack down on the mobile phones. The challenging group exploded in anger at the new regime, offended that Toby was endangering their easy setup. They started to protest saying:

"I thought that you were OK, but you're fake!"

"Why are you being like that? You weren't like that last week?"

The challenging students became fully fledged Disrupters, becoming rowdier than before, leaving Toby stressed and confused. The better-behaved students felt neglected as Toby spent so much time appeasing with the Disrupters and was fed up of the circus that their classroom had become. After two weeks of this disruption, Toby went back to how he was before: jokey and friendly on the surface, but secretly feeling defeated.

The Yo-Yo
Swings Between Dictator and Doormat In A Very Short Period

When I was growing up, I had a Science teacher called Mr Patrick (not his real name), who was, without a shadow of a doubt, the most confusing man that I had ever met. Whenever we knew that his class was next, we all let out a collective groan. Going to Mr Patrick's class was a cross between *Charlie and The Chocolate Factory* and early M. Night Shyamalan film — his lessons were bonkers.

The issue with Mr Patrick wasn't his subject knowledge, as I am persuaded to this day that he was an actual scientific genius. He conducted the most remarkable practical experiments, wowing us with magnesium, water and Bunsen burners.

What was baffling was how he treated his students. Mr Patrick's moods changed at the drop of a penny: one minute he would be laughing because the projector was broken but then, ten seconds later, he would be screaming because someone moved their stool. He was utterly unpredictable, and I hated it.

I was absolutely terrible at Science and everyone knew it. Mr Patrick could spend the whole lesson talking about the differences between Newtonian and Einsteinian physics, with such passion that he would make your head spin in wonder. But then the next day, he would be sullen, moody and scream at the smallest issue. There were days when my friends and I would peak through the door to see what mood he was in — there was no middle ground.

Mr Patrick loved putting people on the spot and he was absolutely ruthless. His finger was like a loaded Colt Magnum 44 pistol and most of the time he would aim it at me. When Mr Patrick asked me, "What is the difference between centripetal acceleration and centrifugal force?" I knew my goose was cooked. I mumbled something about "speed over time" and saw him go scarlet red and with a bellow, scream "GET OUT OF MY CLASS." I was relieved. I couldn't take the tension any longer. While I was outside, enjoying my five minutes of freedom, a confused Mr Patrick asked me why I was standing outside his room. I stared at him blankly and told him that he had sent me out. He went red again and snarled at me to get inside immediately. This was a typical day in Mr Patrick's world, and it drove us, absolutely crazy.

After two years of his rampages, the Disrupters managed to get themselves kicked out of the class, the Complaints staged guerrilla warfare and the Positives and Engaged groaned and tried to cope under this crazy regime. As a grown man, I am still scared of Mr Patrick.

In the first example, Mike didn't even want to climb the Trust Mountain with his students. In Mike's head, he would have been happy if they were all Complaint. But remember what I said in the beginning: Trust Mountain is not fixed, but always in flux, depending on the dynamics in the class. Looking at his class's Trust Mountain, his military strategy took the students that were potential Positives and demotivated them so much that they dropped to become Compliants. Then the potential Compliants became so angry and resentful that they just became Disrupters. He relied on his Positional Authority, but his standoffish and distant nature stopped him from building the Personal Authority that would have made them Positives and Engaged.

In Toby's example, it seemed like at the beginning, he started off really well. He created a warm atmosphere, and on the surface, the majority were Positives. However, in reality, he was appeasing their bad behaviour and not setting any standards. This sent conflicting messages to his pupils, as poor behaviour seemed to be rewarded. The challenging learners who were briefly Positives quickly slipped to Compliants and when challenged, became Disrupters — because they didn't look at Toby as a teacher but a 'mate.' Toby's lack of authority allowed the Disrupters to take over and dominate the room.

Mr Patrick is an example of an exceptional case, called the "Yo-Yo." Yo-Yo teachers can rapidly go between the two extremes often within minutes which bewilder everyone that has to work with them — including their colleagues. This will totally undermine your authority and respect and leave you at the bottom of Trust Mountain.

The reason why I brought up Mr Patrick is as follows. More often than not, no matter how consistent we feel in the class when it comes to dealing with bad behaviour, we can easily fall into the Yo-Yo trap: we come down too heavy on minor disruptions like talking and can be too light on serious ones like aggression and rudeness. By the way, this includes me also — being a teacher is hard graft and something you always have to get better at. To do that we need one magic word — consistency.

Although those three examples are extreme, these are real issues that teachers face today. Throughout my career, I have been both Mike and Toby (and had a sprinkling of Mr Patrick). Despite writing this book, I still have to make sure that I am staying 'centre.' Some days are better than others. But as someone once told me, learning to teach is like driving on a long, straight motorway. Even though you are not doing much, you have to keep your eyes on the road and your hand firmly on the wheel. If you don't, you'll drift and end up upside down in a ditch.

So, what if you don't know your classroom management style?

It happens. Answer these questions honestly - I promise not to peek.

- Do you feel you have to relay the same instructions to the class and they do not listen to you at all?
- Are there cliques of students in your class who feel that the rules do not apply to them?
- Is there constant low-level disruption when you are teaching? Do learners continuously fidget/talk/play with things rather than focus on your agenda?
- Do your students constantly talk over you?
- Do students consistently come late to your lesson and are unapologetic about it?
- Do students take an extremely long time to settle down once the class has started?
- Do your students regularly make comments that provoke you or the other students in the class? When challenged, are they sarcastic or aggressive?

If you have answered 'yes' to the majority of these questions, it may suggest that you haven't built up enough authority and you may have to re-assert your boundaries taking you towards the "Firm" route. The "Bad" and "Ugly" sections of this book will have lots of tips to help you redress the balance.

But let's look at the other side. Take a look at these questions:

- In general, do you feel that your classes tend to be lifeless and dull?
- Do you feel that you have to micromanage the class to get anything done?
- Do have a bucketload of rules that your students must follow?
- Do you find yourself repeatedly shouting and firefighting? (This will be explained later)
- Do your students find it difficult to answer your questions? Are they fearful when you select them for a public task?
- Do your students find you unapproachable?
- Are your students engaged in what you teach? When you have interactive sections of your lesson, are the students reluctant to join in?
- Do your students regularly make excuses to leave the class?
- Do your students display negative body language such as putting their heads on their desk, leaning back in their chairs or avoiding eye-contact with you?

If the second batch of questions look more like your classroom, this could be a sign that your students might be disengaged and unmotivated. In these circumstances, they are just complying with your requests but not engaging with you or the subject. The strategies in the "Good" section of the book can help fire your students up, taking you to the top of the pyramid.

In the next chapter, we will look at your absolute MUST HAVE to help you and your students climb up Trust Mountain. If you master the next chapter, everything else becomes easy. Trust me, you will see.

The Social Contract

The Rules vs The Social Contract

Years ago, when I was training to become a teacher, I remember listening to my wise lecturer and scribbling furiously in my notepad. She was giving one of her famous talks on Classroom Management and I was loving it. This woman had two decades of teaching experience and had literally taught in every kind of environment from prisons to horse stables. She knew her stuff and had the class on the edge of our seats. She always used to say "the backbone of any classroom management strategies are the institute's rules and regulations that must be enforced without fear or trepidation."

As I looked at my NEET (Not in Education, Employment or Training) learners for the first time, I knew I had more of a chance of becoming the US President than getting any of this lot to follow any rules or regulations. There was plenty of fear and trepidation — for me at least.

A mere hour before, my boss and I first entered the study centre, based in East London, where we were going to do an initial assessment of the students for our pilot NEET project.

When I got the job as the NEETs coordinator, I thought that I hit the 'Big Leagues' - I wasn't just teaching, but I was also in charge of shaping the schemes of work and the direction that this course would go. I was working with a great team and now driving a new shiny project that had a good shot at transforming the lives of the students we were to teach. I was making a difference, and it felt great.

Those feelings started to disappear, seemingly through my sweat glands, as we walked through the heavily reinforced structure. The staff were very welcoming and cheerful, almost as if they wanted to offset the stern look of the building.

Everything and I mean everything, was magnetically locked or 'maglocked' in this place. Need to check the Internet? Nope, the computers were maglocked. Need to go to the toilet? Nope, the toilets were maglocked. Need to go into another classroom to talk to someone? Nope, you guessed it, the doors were maglocked. This made the process of getting to the class longer and even more intimidating. What was happening in here? Were they protecting government secrets? Was there a monster in the building that they had to stop from getting into civilisation? Were they hiding the road to El Dorado?

When I finally reached my class, the Youth Worker lead us in there with the nervous smile of a man who was leading sheep into a lion's den. There they were — my bright young charges - and they were not happy. At this time, the UK Government had recently changed the Education policy stating that students could only formally leave formal education when they were eighteen, whereas before it had been sixteen. That meant most students who completed their GCSEs would go to do A-Levels, college qualifications like the BTEC, GNVQs or work-based schemes like paid apprenticeships.

Not our lot. Many of these learners were either permanently excluded from school or simply didn't turn up to do their GCSEs. Looking through my case notes, I could see that many of my students were diagnosed with Social Emotional and Mental Health needs (SEMH), some had learning difficulties like dyslexia and autism and, although it wasn't finalised before we got there, some may have had complex social, emotional and mental challenges like Borderline and Obsessive-Compulsive Personality Disorders.

Because of their poor grades and their behaviour, our students wouldn't be taken by any Further Education institutions. Their outlooks seemed equally bleak: Many of these guys were already members of gangs and were disturbingly familiar with the street and drug culture.

The borough they came from was one of the poorest in the country. These guys would have slipped through the cracks of society and, without intervention, could end up repeating this cycle of low aspiration, violence and despair. This centre for most of them was the last-chance-saloon and our job was to set them on the right path. At the time, this was more than I could handle and I really felt out of my depth.

They were a rough lot. We tried to talk to them but many tended to be unresponsive. Grunts, smirks and one-word answers were their main communication strategies. Although the initial presentation was OK, I knew it would be a rollercoaster ride from here on out.

I have nothing but immense respect for the youth workers and mentors who would sit in our lessons, as I felt that they were often the barrier between some form of order and utter chaos. The first couple of sessions were a little ropey, as many of them could come to class late, be totally unresponsive or do very little work. Emotional outbursts were not uncommon as one student could make a seemingly innocent comment to his friend and the other one would fly into a blind rage, physically having to be restrained or escorted out of the room.

The students wouldn't pay any attention to the rules and the consequences — if sanctioned, they just wouldn't turn up, leaving us stumped in what to do. It wasn't working. They didn't want to be there and we didn't want to either. They didn't want to work and it felt like sometimes we were just hanging in there by the skin of our teeth keeping these guys in the room. My previous experiences in school were not translating well in this environment. I was wondering whether I made a mistake in taking this role.

During a Media lesson, one of the students picked up a metal-cased sound card and threatened to beat the crap out of another student with it. The students were up in arms and we had enough. We took an impromptu break and the Course Director, myself and the other available tutors had an emergency meeting and looked at what we could do to control the situation. The Course Director said it was my call on how we could change things around, and we all felt the pressure. A wise youth worker called Abz said something that not only changed the direction of the course but the way that I dealt with all my students from that point. Abz said, "Just be real with them. Try to understand where they were coming from. Don't talk down to them — ask them what they want out of the classes."

We walked back into the classroom and did just that. I told the students that I could understand how they are feeling. I also told them that I came from another part of East London that was very similar to where they came from. I told them that I knew people that had been murdered, those who had ended up on drugs and are now either homeless or dead. I knew people who hadn't got an education and were just getting by doing petty crimes, living a miserable life.

After I spoke, there was silence. I thought that I said something wrong and I had totally blown it. But one by one, the learners started opening up about their experiences: many felt like schools never gave them a chance and that they were discriminated against because of their backgrounds. Some said that they felt like schools and colleges were 'prisons' and they didn't see the point of going. Some thought that the rules only seemed to apply to the students, not the adults and that many teachers were trying to "bully" them. We all listened attentively — it was the most that a lot of them had said while they had been on the course.

We then asked them how they would like the remainder of the course to run: we asked them how everyone should be treated in the room, how we should work and what type of atmosphere that we wanted to maintain. We worked on this for the rest of the session. Everyone agreed to this 'contract', and that we would try our best to live up to those values. Although that particular class was still tricky, there was a massive improvement in behaviour, and everyone in the room started to enjoy our sessions.

As each year passed, at our college we started to refine our "social contract", and became more confident and assured in our classrooms. I realised that most students wanted the same things: to be respected, to be safe, to be listened to and ultimately, to have fun. The length of time to set up this contract became shorter and shorter, and most of the tutors felt comfortable using it. This was honestly a breakthrough moment in my teaching career and for many of us on these projects.

When I left my NEETs coordinator role, I initially just did supply teaching in secondary schools. I was expecting the classroom management side of things to be different from the NEET level stuff that I had grown used to. I was very shocked to see that it was not only very similar to what I had been doing - in some ways, it was worse.

Supply teaching in Inner City London was eye-opening. Most students look at supply teachers the same way that a hungry lion looks at a terrified gazelle – fresh meat. Learners had absolute contempt for the poor strangers that was filling in for their absent tutors. In the beginning, many of my classes resembled a scene out of *Mad Max: Fury Road* without the cool trucks. I have seen grown men and women reduced to tears after covering lessons in certain schools. There have been many times in the classroom that I felt like

Russell Crowe's Maximus Meridius in *Gladiator* screaming "ARE YOU NOT ENTERTAINED?"

In all sincerity, what has always saved me from the fate of many of my supply teaching colleagues was the Social Contract. Even if I taught a class for one hour, I would religiously spend at least ten minutes writing the classroom expectations on the board while trying to gauge what that class' needs were. This has been my number one tool for classroom management, and although it's simple, it's incredibly useful.

What is a Social Contract?

According to the Cambridge Dictionary, a social contract is, "an agreement among the members of a society or between a society and its rulers about the rights and duties of each[10]." This isn't merely setting ground rules; you are entering an agreement with your students on how you are going to work together. You are establishing your authority, yet you are also showcasing your emotional intelligence by showing that you value your students' input. A question that you may ask next could be, "Why can't I just get the institution's rules and put them on the board?" Good question. Let's go through the reasons why.

1) The School Rules are very broad. The Social Contract that you set with the class will be very specific to your students' needs.

I live in London, England which and is a part of the United Kingdom (UK). The UK has many great laws like not killing your neighbours and stealing other people's cars. However, over the thousands of years of our rich history, we have developed several strange rules that still apply today. Don't believe me? In 2016, UK-based newspaper *The Independent* published a list of most unusual statutes including:

- It is an offence to be drunk and in charge of cattle in England and Wales
- It is illegal to jump the queue in the Tube ticket hall
- It is an offence to beat or shake any carpet, rug, or mat (except doormats before 8am) in a thoroughfare in the Metropolitan Police District
- It is illegal to handle a salmon in suspicious circumstances
- It is illegal to be drunk in the pub[11]

I have broken at least three out of five of those rules (how could you handle a salmon under suspicious circumstances?) The reasons why they may look ridiculous is because a) they are not relevant and b) we cannot understand the context in which these laws were devised and why they should be enforced.

These are extreme examples and I not saying that your institution's rules are irrelevant. But what I am saying is the Social Contract should cater specifically to your learners' needs.

Some of you may disagree. Some of you may feel that behaviour management is up to the institution and not your concern. Your job is to teach and that's it, nothing more, nothing less. Well, I'm sorry to burst your bubble, but that is about as true as Arsenal winning the Champions League. No matter your thoughts on your institution's behaviour policy, your class' behaviour is YOUR responsibility and if something happens in YOUR class, YOU will be held responsible. Besides if your institution's behaviour policy is non-existent, then I think it is time for you to leave and get another job. It's not worth the stress.

Take ownership and look at ways that you can make life better for you and your students.

2) The Rules are fixed and set by the institution, and you cannot easily change them. The Social Contract is set by you and your class, and everybody is welcome to contribute.

Your institution's rules were developed to be in line with the Government's Education Teaching Standards. I have no issue with that, as we must hold ourselves to the highest professional requirements. As teachers, we must make sure that we follow the rules of our institutions.

But remember, no one will know the needs of your class than better than you, the teacher. Each institution you work in will have its own unique challenges that you can address from the get-go. This also gives your students a unique opportunity: the chance to have a say in how the classroom is run and feel that they are being listened to. This is powerful, as you will show their feelings matter and if they feel involved, they are more likely to follow what you create.

3) The School Rules relies on compliance. The Social Contract encourages cooperation and engagement.

I have taught across the spectrum and whether they are in nervous nine olds in Year Five or rebellious seventeen-year-olds in Year Twelve, over the years I have heard the same complaint — "Why do we have to follow the rules when the teachers break them all the time?"

The Social Contract should be upheld by EVERYONE in the class.

It's a two-way street. The Social Contract not only applies to our students but it applies to us as well. If you have a "no mobile phone" policy in the classroom and you sit there looking at your Snapchat story, then you completely undermine what you are striving to achieve.

Remember this key point:

Humans do not follow rules, they follow people.

If your students see that you are someone who has integrity and is a person of their word, you will gain their respect and trust. The Social Contract is an opportunity for the class to get to know you and vice-versa. If this is done right, you are signal to your group that you are someone worth following. Try not to be a hypocrite.

I don't know where you are teaching but here in London, we boast one of the most diverse communities in the UK. I regularly teach students with cultural roots from every corner of the globe. Each student brings with them their own social norms, cultures, religions, family dynamics and values into the classroom.

The Social Contract allows you to create a set of standards that you can all stand behind, no matter what background or position you have.

I know that on the surface, this process may look simple and even juvenile. I know that spelling out basic rules, especially for our older learners, may seem like we are patronising them. Do it anyway. The rewards outweigh the risks and could be the birth of something beautiful in your class. To use the great David Cameron quote, "we are all in this together", and you will mean it.

Besides I can put my Friday night pizza money on the fact that you would not be reading this book if making them follow the School Rules wasn't a problem...

How To Set Up The Social Contract

The Americans have the US Constitution. The British have the Magna Carta. The United Nations have the Universal Declaration of Human Rights. Now your class will have the Social Contract. The Social Contract will become the glue that will bind your group together. Whatever you agree on, will become the law of the land. The Social Contract is your basecamp to help you climb up Trust Mountain. This will develop into the backbone of your classroom management strategies, and this will set the standards of everyone in the class. If you don't establish this contract, all the other parts of this book will be as much use as a car that is made out of jelly: messy and pointless.

Take time to read through this section and PUT THIS SECTION INTO ACTION. If you do this correctly, you will thank me for it. Practice this on every class until you know it like the back of your hand.

Initially, it may take ten to fifteen minutes to get the contract up and running. But once you are used to how it works, you can do this in five minutes tops. When your students first walk through the door, get them settled and then walk them through these steps.

Step 1 - Ask Them For Their Input

Introduce the exercise by asking them for their opinions. You could say something along the lines of:

- "The Social Contract is designed so that we can all work in a more harmonious environment and I need your input."
- "This is the first time that we have met, and I wanted to put something in place to make sure that we all understand each other's boundaries and we can work better together"
- "I've noticed that in the lessons so far, we haven't been as positive towards each other as we could have been. I want to put something together that will help this class become better for everyone, and I need your thoughts."

THE SOCIAL CONTRACT

You get the picture. In most cases in my teaching career, most students are receptive if you ask for their opinions and will be willing to hear you out. If you do get the odd student who is being silly or disrespectful, or persistently disruptive, then they can be sent somewhere else until the exercise is done. This is a very critical time and you must assert your authority; otherwise you will lose the class.

Step 2 - Explain what the Social Contract is

Very briefly explain the Social Contract is. It can be as simple or complex as you like. You could say something along the lines of:

- "The Social Contract is an agreement between every single person in the room, teacher or student, on how to treat each other and how we work together."
- "The Social Contract is a set of rules that we will design together that will ensure that everyone in the room will feel safe and positive while we are in the class."
- "The Social Contract is a chance for all of us to have a say on how our classroom is run."

Another great tip that has helped me over the years is to explain that we live in a society that is full of social contracts and we already know some. Use the restaurant example: unless they raised in a box, most students know that, if they enter a restaurant, they do not take food off strangers' plates without asking for permission. This example usually gets them to understand that they already have an idea of how to behave in wider society and we can transfer that into the classroom.

Step 3 - Write their Suggestions on the Board

At this point, write their inputs on the board. If they are still struggling to come up with some suggestions, ask them the following:

- "What things could we do to make this a positive environment for everyone?"
- "How do you want to be treated and how do you think other

people would like to treated?"
- "What things could we do so that everyone feels included and welcomed into our class?"
- "What things do you *not* want to happen in the class and why?"

They may say things like "no fighting" or "we shouldn't speak over each other" — just write them down. Use shorthand — try and encapsulate the essence of the rule in a couple of words, a sentence at the most. Depending on the age and how tricky the class is, you may get one or two suggestions to a thousand answers being fired at you. That is fine, as long as it's under control and you can get the most important rules on the board. This shouldn't take more than three minutes to complete.

Step 4 - Get Everyone To Agree To These Rules Verbally

Once you have covered all the main rules and the students have no more to contribute to the board, tell them that this is now the final draft of the contract and if anyone is not satisfied then they must raise their hand. Give the class thirty seconds to respond. Do not neglect to do this.

Several things are happening at that moment. By asking that question, you are placing power back in the students' hands, and they now have to make a choice. If this part is done correctly, then most of your class will agree with what you have written on the board. Any naysayers will have to explain why they are going against the wishes of the majority of the class and have to articulate why.

This can be a great moment. You and your students can have a dialogue on what works and what doesn't, and you can gain a greater understanding of your pupils' motivations. This also adds social pressure on those who may step out of line.

If there are students that are absolutely adamant that they will not follow any of these rules, then you will have to employ some in the strategies in the "Bad" and "Ugly" sections. If they are polite, then after you set the tasks, take them to one side and talk to them about it and try to understand their objections. But if they are rude

THE SOCIAL CONTRACT

and defiant, then they are already showing you that they will not cooperate and you will have to draw your line in the sand.

Once you have completed the final draft, make sure the Social Contract is on display AT ALL TIMES. I don't care if you write it on the corner of the board, make a poster, get Fred Flintstone to engrave it into the wall, it doesn't matter. Every time something happens in the class, you will need to refer back to these rules. The Social Contract is your friend; give it the respect that it deserves.

The Social Contract Template

If you are still unsure whether you're doing it right, then have no fear! I have provided the Social Contract that I still use with my classes today to act as your template. Edit it as you see fit. Most of the core aspects of the Social Contract can be captured under these main headings. When I walk into a new classroom, I use this framework to help me create the Social Contract rapidly and now you can too. Here's a point by point explanation.

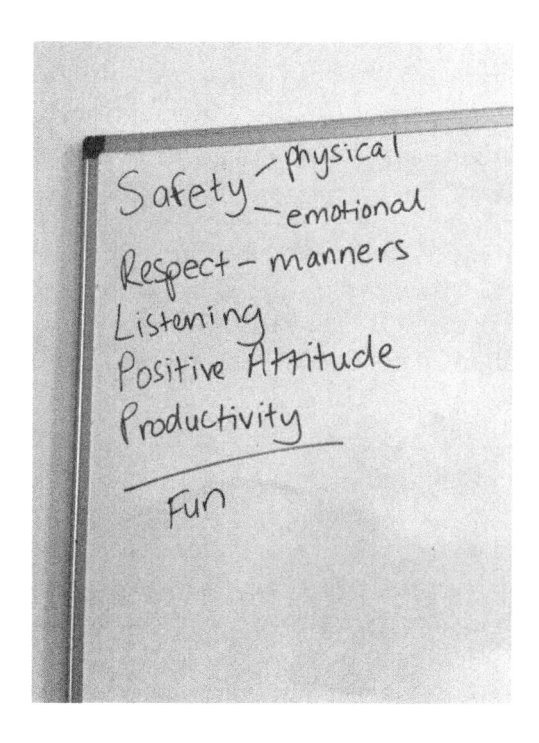

Safety

Rule numero uno. Explain to the class that none of the other rules will work if we cannot feel safe. Safety is composed of two parts:

- **Physical Safety** - No-one in the class should touch others in a way that makes them feel uncomfortable or threatened.

This includes the obvious culprits such as punching, kicking, slapping and prodding, but this also includes unwanted hugs, touching others inappropriately and caressing.

- **Emotional Safety -** No-one in the class should say things that will intentionally hurt other people's feelings. Make it very clear that no-one should mock people based on their colour, religion, gender, sexuality, financial status, nationality or anything else. More often than not, a violation of emotional safety will lead directly to someone's physical safety being threatened. When I was growing up in East London, a sure way to get into a fight with someone was to insult his or her mother. All someone had to say was "Your Mum", and several fists would come flying their way. You must emphasise that every single person must feel welcome in the class – no exceptions.

Of all the rules, this one must be upheld and cherished. Remember Maslow's Hierarchy of Needs? Which need was right at the bottom? Yep, physical safety. If you cannot guarantee the safety of your students, then good luck doing anything else with them.

Respect

This is the second most important rule in the classroom. In inner city London, the students are very fond of talking about this concept. If you have you ever heard cries of "Nah, don't disrespect me!" Then you get the idea. Respect determines how you speak to each other and treat each other in the room. As the Golden Rule states, "do unto others as you want others to do unto you." Tell your students to speak to everyone in the room how they want to be spoken to. Explain to your students that as long as everyone shows good manners towards each other, then this rule is easy to uphold.

Listening

This one is an easy one. Every person in the class deserves to be heard, whether they are the students or the teachers. Teach your students to use "active listening" and explain why it is important. I love the definition that author Rodrigo Ortiz Crespo presents in his book *The Active Listener*. Crespo states "Active Listening represents a physical and mental effort to carefully understand the whole message...showing the speaker through feedback what we have believed that we understood." [12]

Tell your students that listening carefully and thoughtfully shows the other person that you care about their opinion. Especially with the younger students, go over ways to show people that you are listening to them like eye contact, not speaking over others and how their bodies should be turned towards the speaker. Adjust this rule for your needs.

Positive Attitude

This rule refers to how the individual's presence affects everyone around them and how everyone in the room must be mindful of their demeanour towards others.

Talk to your students about how body language, tone of voice and their movement styles can be perceived as either positive or negative and model what will make people feel comfortable in class. But explain the caveat. This doesn't necessarily mean that your students must lie about how they feel or be 'happy-go-lucky' all the time. We all have bad days. However, their attitude should not, to the best of their ability, make others feel unsafe or uncomfortable in the classroom.

Productivity

This rule is crucial to emphasise. Explain to your class that everyone has to do the work to the best of their abilities. With this particular rule, you may find a little resistance, but if you do a lot of the things in the "Good" section then you can ease the burden!

Make your students see the big picture: whether it is to pass their GCSEs, gain their apprenticeship, or enter university, the class' job is to work together to make that dream a reality. Notice that I framed it as "working to best of *our* ability." From our teacher training, we know how to differentiate. Do not be afraid to push and challenge your students — they are not in your institution for a free ride.

Fun

Explain to your students that overall, everyone should enjoy the lesson. Study after study has shown that fun helps you learn faster — why do you think kids love computer games? Fun is a result of peace and harmony. But there is a line underneath that word. **Your students must understand that no-one can have fun until all the other parts of the contract are completed, it's that simple.**

So, let's do a quick recap:

1. You've learnt what the Trust Mountain is, what two aspects you need to climb it and what pitfalls you need to avoid.
2. You've learnt what the Social Contract is, how this differs from your organisation's rules and how to set up your own version.

Well done people! We've reached the end of your mandatory reading. In the next couple of sections, we will look at the individual strategies and tips that you can use in your classroom. Remember, that these strategies won't work unless you do. Try one for a couple of days at least and if it doesn't work then go on to the next one, no biggie. Let's go.

The Good

Give them Praise

Nobody likes being criticised. If you want to encourage your students, practice praising them instead. "Praise the slightest improvement and praise every improvement. Be hearty in your approbation and lavish in your praise."[1] That quote came from the timeless classic *How To Win Friends And Influence People* by Dale Carnegie, and has served me wonderfully over the years. This works very well on every level of Trust Mountain because most people respond positively to encouragement. So why is praising your students important? Here are a couple of reasons:

- It makes your students feel valued and appreciated
- It creates a positive environment for your classroom
- It helps them to build confidence

But there is a catch: If you think that praising people is merely brown-nosing, then you are sadly mistaken. Our students' BS readers are finely tuned, and they will know if you're being insincere. When you are praising your students, here are a couple of tips to make sure that you don't sound like a used car salesperson.

- Praise them for their effort, *not* their ability — our natural instinct, when we see our students excel in our subject, is to say that they are 'gifted' or they are 'brilliant' – but this could cause more harm than good. Studies have shown that students praised based only on their abilities, will become *more demotivated* over time. These students become anxious, fearing every mistake and knockback as a poor reflection on them as an individual and not an event that happens to us all. This causes 'performance anxiety', negative states of mind and can lead to poor mental health. As we all know, mistakes are an unavoidable part of learning and something we should embrace rather than dread. Dr Carol Dweck suggests that we should use something called "process praise" instead. Dweck writes that this type of praise "conveys to students that they can develop their abilities and it suggests how this can be done. We find that it makes children more likely to want

challenging work and to persist when the work gets more difficult."[2] Praise them for their effort first and then look at their results.
- Know what types of praise that your students respond to — once you get to know your students you will learn how they like to be praised. Praise them in the way that would they prefer. For example, some learners may react well when they are praised privately rather than in front of everyone in the class.
- Praise them quickly and get to the point — in my personal experience, if you do a song and dance when you praise your students, this could lose its effect and embarrass them. Catch them doing something right and compliment them on the spot. Keep it tight and short.

So, praise is great but… does that mean that we should never correct our students? Not quite. Praise can be even used to challenge and check your students if necessary - my personal go-to is the "Crap Sandwich." (I know there is a more alliterative name for this, but you all know why I can't print it in this book.)

The Crap Sandwich

The 'Crap Sandwich' model is as follows: When critiquing your student's work, highlight a positive element of what they have done right, then look at the area to improve (feedback), and then end it on another positive aspect. Here's an example:

POSITIVE: John I love the way that used metaphors and similes in your creative writing task and your story was really engaging.

FEEDBACK: Your work would be even better if we just made sure that we are using the correct punctuation and double-checking your spellings as well.

POSITIVE: Overall you have written three sides of work and I know how much effort you put into this task. Good job!

What is great about this model is that it allows you to give feedback to your students in a non-threatening way, so that keeps their motivation levels high. Also, the fact that you are finding something positive to say shows that on some level, you care about their feelings.

When the Crap Sandwich is NOT appropriate

The Crap Sandwich is not a cure-all — there are situations where this will just not work. If you have a conversation with Johnny Tableflipper and he well… flips a table, you can't say:

"Johnny I love the way you flipped the table, you did manage to break my arm and my spirit, but I appreciate your energy and enthusiasm, great job!"

I would be worried about your sanity if you thought that was OK. If that happened, then you are in what I would call a 'flashpoint' situation — this is something that grinds all classroom learning to a halt. Emotions will be riding high, and your students will not be in the mood to hear your feedback. If you find yourself facing a flashpoint, you will need to use more robust tactics. Check "The Ugly" section for more details.

Reflection Questions

1. Do you regularly praise your students? If you don't, why not? How will your students react to your praise?
2. If you do praise your students, when do you do it and why? Are you recognising your students based on their abilities or their efforts? Do you differentiate your praise?
3. Do you find yourself praising the same groups of students? Why is that? Are there any ways you can open it up to other students in the class?

Practical Tips

- Pick one student who you don't interact with as much as the others. Observe them over your next lesson. If they are working hard, attempting difficult tasks with a positive attitude or working well with their peers, then sincerely give them some praise. It can be as short as five seconds. Short, sharp and to the point.

- This is a good Jedi mind-trick that one of my colleagues taught me and uses reverse psychology. If a student hasn't done something that you have requested them to do, praise them in front of their peers as if they have already done it. For example, there was a Year 10 boy called Charlie who was in my colleague's class and would never take his jacket off when he entered the room. Rather than badger him to remove his coat continually, my colleague would merely say "Thank you Charlie for taking off your jacket" and smile. Charlie would apologise and immediately do just that without argument. It never ceases to amaze me how effective that technique is. Try it and see!

- During a flashpoint situation, the Crap Sandwich won't be helpful but can be useful AFTER the incident has taken place, and can be used as part of a restorative meeting. Here's an example: two male Year 10 students had a pushing match in your classroom and had to be removed by another teacher. You handled the flashpoint, the sanctions were given and now you want to do some form of a restorative meeting with the boy who started the fight. If there are still any issues or 'beefs', you can use LAST (see the "Ugly" section). Once you have passed that hurdle, you can use the Crap Sandwich to deliver your feedback about his behaviour.

POSITIVE: First of all, I want to say well done for calming yourself down, explaining the situation in a calm manner and apologising for the disruption you caused in my class. That is appreciated.

FEEDBACK: As we both agreed, the argument in the class should not have happened. This disrupted the learning and you missed out on a critical section that would have helped you in the exam. Because of that, you served the sanction of [insert sanction here]. If there is a problem in future, you speak to me first.

POSITIVE: Max, I have taught you for a long time, and I know how good you can be in the class. I know how disciplined, focused and polite you are with everyone around you and I know that you

THE GOOD

can return to that level. I have faith that we can put this behind us and have a better lesson tomorrow.

When you are using the Crap Sandwich in this case, notice that there is more "meat" between your buns — this is because you have lots more feedback to deliver! But rather than ending the lesson on a sour note, you have at planted the seeds of a better experience next time.

Have a Sense of Humour

Comedy is a massive business. In 2015, *The Evening Standard* reported that the UK Comedy Industry is worth "£400m a year. Many of the country's top comedians are overtaking Premier League footballers in earning power, thanks to sell-out stadium tours, TV appearances, DVD sales and book deals[3]." That is some serious wonga. People like to laugh and smile — it makes us feel good. I am sure that many teaching academics would be absolutely horrified at what I'm suggesting — smiling in the classroom? Enjoyment during lessons? Preposterous!

But before you get your monocles in a twist, there has been a lot of scientific research that has explained why humour can beneficial and why we live in a time that a stand-up comedian can command as much money as music superstar like Beyoncé.

Why Humour?

Before I talk about why humour could be an essential tool in your classroom arsenal, let's try to answer the basics: why do like humour? From an evolutionary perspective, why do we find humour attractive? Psychologist Shawn Achor believes that humour is a sign of one's 'cognitive fitness.' Achor writes that humour shows that "your brain must be flexible, quick, and sharp to comprehend or create humour. The funniest people are those that can see a version of reality, the rest of us might miss[4]."

The best comedians force us to look at the world differently: using humour to help us navigate life's many mysteries, struggles and contradictions — that takes incredible brainpower. Here are a couple of advantages to having good humour.

- Stress relief — whenever we laugh, we produce a chemical in our brain called dopamine. This hormone helps us to feel good and helps us to relax.
- Boosts morale — when balanced with respect, humour can help you create a positive atmosphere in your class, making it a more pleasant place to work in. In times of stress such

as exam periods or coursework deadlines, this can help keep your class's spirits up.
- Facilitates trust — ultimately, having a good sense of humour shows that you are a human being and not an android. This enables people to trust you and helps build the rapport between you and all the other individuals in your class.

Humour in the Classroom

Let's be clear: I am not asking any of you to become Chris Rock, Eddie Izzard or Tina Fey here: humour has the massive potential to backfire too. If you do it the wrong way, you will lose some of that authority that you have worked so hard to create… and possibly your job. Here are a couple of guidelines to keep you kosher.

- Keep it professional — different ages respond to varying types of humour, but remember we are in a place of work and we are bound by a set of professional standards. Keep it clean folks and use the "Line Manager Test": if my manager was in the classroom, would I be happy to say this sentence? If not, then bin it.
- Keep it light and short — if you launch into a full-blown Netflix special, you will not get any brownie points with your employers, and you won't get any work done.
- Context is key — be inclusive. Especially if you are a diverse class, please remember what one group finds funny, another group may offensive. I have seen people throw punches over a bad joke about their football team. Be sensitive and learn your learners' likes and dislikes over time.
- Be kind - use humour to uplift people, not roast them. Many great comedians are absolute masters at this style of comedy such as Ellen Degeneres, James Corden, the late Bruce Forsyth. Their humour made people feel good about themselves and made everyone feel more at ease. If you use your humour to demean, embarrass or humiliate your students, you are creating a rod for your own back.

The aim of this chapter is not to make you a stand-up comedian but to help you realise that the right balance of humour can make your class a better place. Even if you don't feel comfortable using humour in your teaching, the reality is that some of your students will have more enhanced comedic chops than others. That's why having a 'sense' of humour is vital: if you try to eradicate it from your classroom completely, this may come out in disruptive behaviour patterns.

The same rules apply to your students too. If they are respectful, kind and they don't override your lesson why not let a bit of humour in your class? You may find allowing them express themselves improves their behaviour. If your students go too far, this is a great way to reintroduce elements of the Social Contract and to make clear what the boundaries are.

Reflection Questions

1. Do you feel you have to be constantly stern with your students? Is your classroom humourless? If so, why? Are there places where you could use humour to break the tension?
2. Can your students express their own sense of humour in the class? Is it disruptive or positive? How do you usually respond?
3. If you already use humour in the classroom, could you be *overusing* it? Why is that? What ways could you counterbalance this?

Practical Tips

- Humour is all about positivity — even if you don't use it, sometimes it's all about smiling and taking things in your stride. Next time something goes wrong in your class, rather than get aggravated, smile, take a deep breath and keep on going — it shows confidence.
- If you have any budding comedians, see if you can use their gifts rather than rather than suppress them. Once you have

THE GOOD

> built up a bit of trust, get them more involved in your activities. Make them the spokesperson in a debate or get them to write a speech. Think outside the box and make their energy useful. You may be the only teacher that shows appreciation for their gifts, and that will take you higher on their Trust Mountain. But you must remind them that they have to stick to the Social Contract and everything else in this chapter.

- Sometimes, as you may know, students can use humour for darker purposes. Some students use humour to embarrass, humiliate and harass others. These students get their kicks from making other peoples' lives a living hell and when confronted, will dismiss their concerns as "banter" and their accusers as "being sensitive." This is usually the weapon of choice for Passive Disrupters (see the chapter "Positives, Compliants and Disrupters" for more details.) This type of humour is bullying, pure and simple. These types of jokers need to be told that their behaviour is not appropriate and that goes against the Social Contract you created. If they continue, then take them outside and offer them "The Easy Road or The Hard Road" (see Be Just, Fair and Firm for more details). This type of humour is abuse and if taken too far, can be devastating mentally and emotionally on the victim. Also, try to keep an eye out for the students that could be targeted for this treatment and help them where necessary.

Cast a Vision

At Feltham Community College, West London, a dedicated PE teacher named Alan Watkinson was trying to persuade one of his students, an energetic thirteen-year-old boy named Mohammad, to take up running full-time rather than take up his childhood dream of playing football. Alan in an interview stated "He was football mad — but he was never going to make it as a footballer and I had to point it out to him. He's a big Arsenal supporter and used to play as a right back but couldn't make the school team." [5] But Alan saw something special in him and eventually, Mohammad started to see it too.

Mohammad was a very gifted runner, but he didn't have it easy. Mohammad was eight years old when he left Somalia after the country descended into a deadly civil war to the hustle and bustle of London, England. Although his father was a long-term resident in the UK, Mohammad struggled to adjust to this strange new environment. Because he was different, he found himself getting into fights and in trouble at the school. Things weren't looking up for the young lad.

Alan met him three years later when he attended Feltham Community College and despite his tough exterior, saw his potential, so he started to invest heavily in him.

Over the years, Alan became a mentor to Mohammad, helping him to hone his running skills, driving him to competitions and even helping him to get travel visas so that he could attend elite training camps abroad. Alan regularly told Mohammad what he could be, painting a great future for him and with each race, he started to believe it too.

Mohammad started climbing the middle-distance running rankings, taking trophy after trophy with Alan by his side. Almost twenty years later, Mohammad did become the Olympic Champion and went on to do it many times more.

If you have not already guessed it, that young man's full name is Sir Mohammad "Mo" Farrah, double 2012 and 2016 Olympic Champion and World Champion over the 5000m and 10,000m distances. Sir Mo has gone on to become a global icon, charity ambassador and Britain's most successful track athlete ever. Alan stated, "I took him aside and told him that if he stuck at running, he could one day compete for Britain. It isn't the sort of thing you say to a kid lightly — it can create unrealistic expectations. But I'm very glad to have been proved right. I'm incredibly proud of him."[6]

It is easy to overlook what we do as teachers in the daily whirlwind of tasks to complete but whether you believe it or not we are in the business of changing lives. You may feel that you are only a teacher, but to some of your students they may see you as a:

- Mentor
- Guide
- Coach
- Role Model
- Surrogate Parent

What Alan did was for Mo was 'Cast a Vision' which gave Sir Mo, despite his present difficulties, a positive picture of his future and helped to give him the push to reach it. Science already has a name for this technique, and it's called the 'Pygmalion Effect.'

The Pygmalion Effect

Psychologists Lenore Jacobson and Robert Rosenthal covered the Pygmalion Effect in a pioneering research study in the Sixties, and this looked at how teachers' beliefs in students affect their performance.

The Pygmalion Effect was named after the character Pygmalion, who happened to star in his own ancient Greek myth. In the story, Pygmalion was a famous sculptor and his creations were revered all over the land. One day, good old Pygmalion created a sculpture of a woman who was so lifelike that he fell in love with it and refused to look at any other woman — very creepy. Poor Pyg, upset and depressed, wished that the statue whom he called Galatea could come to life and be his wife. Aphrodite, the Goddess of Love, was so impressed with Pygmalion's devotion that she granted his wish and Galatea leapt into his arms as a flesh and blood woman. They lived happily ever after, which is lovely but still creepy.

In a controlled experiment, the researchers conducted a series of IQ tests with a primary school class and collected the results. They then informed their teachers that 20% of the students were "gifted" and that later in the year, their academic achievements will outpace that of their classmates. The teachers were given their names. The teachers assumed that the gifted 20% represented the most intellectually talented members of their class and they were treated accordingly, being given more help, more resources and more encouragement.

After eight months, these students indeed did become the top of their classes academically achieving what was predicted. What the teachers did not know was that this was a red herring: the students were chosen entirely at random, with some of them being in the lower half of the class in terms of IQ, but, regardless of their actual ability, still rose to the top. The researchers noted "the results of the experiment further evidence that one's expectations of another's behaviour may come to serve as a self-fulling prophecy[7]." Just as Pyg's belief in Galatea brought her to life, your beliefs about your students, good or bad, can come true too.

Create Leaders

Sometimes you may find yourself in a position where you may have a student who is unreceptive, and they are right at the bottom of the Trust Mountain — they may disrupt your class and cause you to bang your head against the whiteboard in frustration. Does that mean that you shouldn't Cast a Vision? No, not at all — in fact, I believe if you play your cards right, you can develop a leader.

Abraham Lincoln apparently said, "the best way to destroy an enemy is to make him a friend." Wise man Abe was right: sometimes our students lash out because they don't believe in themselves. Some of our students think that they have been written off by society and that there is no hope. But like the old masters in the martial arts movies, you can turn that young grasshopper into a mighty warrior.

The students that disrupt your class do not operate in a vacuum. In my years of experience, one characteristic that I have seen is that many Disrupters is they are not afraid to put themselves forward and get noticed. Some of the most disruptive students that I have ever known have also been the most charismatic. These types have the 'gift of the gab', can talk themselves out of any situation and seem nonplussed at almost anything that gets thrown their way.

Although it is not fun when these students misbehave, they possess some of the qualities that could potentially make them great leaders. Rather than trying to squash these traits out of them, we as teachers should encourage them to use it in a more positive light.

If you have such a character in your class, try to see if they have a particular strength in an area of your subject. If your students are good at something, ask them to give a little talk or organise a task around this ability. Catch them doing something good and praise them about it. If they have got a talent, acknowledge it and champion their development. Push them to become a better version of themselves and hold them to account.

Over time, many of these students rise to your challenge, and they start to embody all the values and the standards that you have set for the class. Once they see their own potential, their newfound discipline and motivation will seep into other areas of their life. It's a joy to watch.

Creating Leaders in Action

When I was a Teaching Assistant in a primary school, just before I started my teacher training, I was given what a small group of five Year 6 students. My job was to provide English booster lessons before they went to secondary school.

These ten-year-olds were flunking their English classes and as it stood, would utterly fail their Key Stage 2 tests, which would hurt their chances in secondary school. The group consisted of boys only and their behaviour was terrible: they were repeatedly being thrown out of classes because they were rude, defiant and even aggressive to their teachers. This was a tall order but the hope was being in a smaller group, would help them focus and settle down.

On the first day, these kids were just not with it at all: one boy put his black Nike Air Maxes on the desk and just sat in the chair with his hands behind his head and smiled smugly at me. I couldn't throw them out of my class as no-one would take them! I am sure the other teachers were having a party when they were with me. After I relayed my concerns to the Assistant Headteacher, she gingerly patted me on the back and told me to 'persevere'.

However, after a couple of sessions with these boys, an interesting pattern started to develop. They thought that there was no point in trying in school as they have "always been dumb, always been bad and that will never change." When I asked them where these labels had come from, many told me that while they were growing up, many authority figures such as teachers and parents had told them that they would "never amount to anything" and even when they tried to change, they were never acknowledged nor taken seriously. I started realising that they had poor self-esteem from the years of discouragement and this was 'playing out' in their behaviour.

I knew that I had to make some changes. I re-dubbed the group 'The Scholars Class' and I told them by the end of the year if they worked hard and they tried their best, they could all pass their tests.

In the small room that I had, I made sure that there were lots of motivational posters and asked them to look at them every day. I gave them short motivational speeches before each lesson about hard work, dedication and grit, and asked them to embody those characteristics. I challenged them to read and write more and lavished praise upon them when they pushed past their comfort zone.

Slowly but surely, these boys started to believe in themselves too, beginning to catch up with the rest of their peers in the standard classes. Five out of the six boys managed to pass their Key Stage 2 tests, which was a great achievement for them and a real watershed moment in my teaching career.

We certainly cannot save every single student that crosses our path and Alan and Sir Mo's story is once in a lifetime event. But you potentially could be the most influential figure in your student's life. History is littered with stories of how great mentors unlocked the genius of their students from

- Johann Cruyff to Pep Guardiola
- Maya Angelou to Oprah Winfrey
- Socrates to Plato

You may never get a famous student, but I can guarantee this: if you are a great teacher you may change the destiny of your pupil's life for the better forever. How cool is that?

Reflection Questions

1. How do your students address themselves? What labels do they use for themselves when it comes to their education? When they use these labels, how do you respond?
2. Do your students have any special abilities or talents? Have you "cast a vision" with them, showing them a bright future if they harness those abilities? Is there any way that you could get them to showcase their talents in your lessons?
3. Do you know your students' career aspirations? Have you made time to talk about their futures? Can you help them create a map from where they are now to where they want to be?

Practical Tips

- You really can't fake this stuff. If you try, they will see right through you. Find a student whom you haven't had a good working relationship with and ask them what they want to do with their life. Take a genuine interest in them and be gentle: they are giving you access to their dreams — don't trample on them.
- You can also use this "vision casting" to challenge your students. If you have a student who, after they have told you their aspirations, doesn't perform to the standard, remind them of what they said they wanted to be and push them to raise their standards to achieve it. Their dreams can act as their 'North Star' which can help keep them focused and diligent.
- Of course, be pragmatic too. When you are casting a vision, there has to be a clear roadmap of where your students want to go. If a student says that he wants to go "inside the sun," then they are being unrealistic. Gently guide them towards

something that is achievable. As that great man Ben Parker, once said "With Great Power Comes Great Responsibility." Use a lot of tact and emotional intelligence.

- Some of you may teach a subject that particular student may not see the point of doing, especially if it is unrelated to what they want to do for a career. Be creative — try to build connections between your subject and what they want to do and why it will help them. There was a boy that I taught who wanted to do football but hated Spanish lessons and wouldn't do any work. The vision I cast for him was that when he was a successful footballer, he may want to go the La Liga - the Spanish Premier League and it would be great if he knew fluent Spanish to talk to his new fans there. I will speak about 'bridging' in future chapters.

Don't Be Boring

Years ago, when I was a telecoms account manager, we were sent away by our company to a 'training camp' usually in a remote part of the country where we would be taught everything to do with our industry. This would often be a mix of small intimate workshops and large concert hall seminars where we learnt everything from sales, customer psychology and the latest technological advances from the best in the industry.

This was an all-expenses-paid trip, where they would put us up in a swanky hotel, and we had a substantial food (and drinks) allowance. We were out of our usual work environments — sounds like we were living the dream, right? Wrong. Apart from my biannual trip to the dentist, this was the event that I tried my hardest to avoid. Why?

It was boring.

Not boring like waiting-in-the-line-at-your-local-supermarket boring, it was boring like is-this-what-purgatory-feels-like-and-I-want-to-cease-to-exist boring. The primary facilitator seemed like he had a major operation to remove every ounce of humour from his body. This lifeless man spoke in a tone that would have made HAL9000 want to go to self-terminate, and I was in a state of perma-sleep in his classes. The other workshops weren't any better — manned by experts who spoke with the excitement of a person that had to go out and buy a can of beans on a Monday morning and spoke with so much jargon that only Scotty from *Star Trek* could understand.

I spent many of my days during the conference desperately trying to understand what was being said, doodling on my notepad, thinking about lunch and stabbing myself in my leg with a pen to stay awake. I almost felt like I was being punished for all the bad things that I did when I was little kid and I couldn't wait to get back to my day job. Have you ever had that experience?

Now I want you to imagine how your students must feel as they navigate our institutions on a day-to-day basis. For some of our students, this can be their daily version of hell where they are shuffled to lessons where they have little understanding of the subject, the delivery is uninspiring and they don't see how any of what they learn will help them with their life.

I know that you already have a lot of things to do and I don't expect your lessons to become as exciting as a Jay-Z concert — the fireworks alone would breach the Health and Safety Rules. But what I am asking you to do is reflect upon your practice and look at whether your students can engage with the material that they are being presented.

If the students find it hard to stay awake in your classroom, then they will find other means to entertain themselves and that would usually involve disrupting your lesson. Some subjects lend themselves to be more 'exciting' than others, but this is where you can get creative — look at ways to innovate and turn your subject matter on its head. Here are three practical tips that have helped me keep my students engaged.

1) Use Stories

Human beings love stories and that is something that has been encoded into our DNA.

In terms of human history, the widespread use of books and papers for the masses to read is a relatively new occurrence starting over 500 years ago. Most of our information was passed down orally usually in story form for thousands of years and we still love it to this day. Robert Rosen, former Dean of the University of California's Theatre, Film and Television faculty stated, "stories put all the key facts into an emotional context… The information in a story doesn't have to sit there in a logical proposition. Instead, it's built to create suspense[8]."

Facts can be stale on their own, but stories have suspense, drama and tension — making it easier to remember and allowing your listeners to connect emotionally with the subject matter. Great stories will make your teaching feel more real and alive. If you want to become better at telling stories that help you influence and persuade people, I wholeheartedly recommend Peter Guber's book *Tell To Win*. Guber's CV is impressive: as the former chairman of Sony Pictures, he produced critically acclaimed hits like *Rain Man*, *A*

Few Good Men and *Sleepless in Seattle* to name a few. One of Guber's guiding film making principles has been that the 'story' is the lifeblood of any movie. If the story sucks, then no actor, director or screenwriter can stop the film being a box-office disaster. I am going to paraphrase Guber's 'Story Framework'[9] and how you can use it in your lessons.

FIRST - get your listeners' attention with an unexpected challenge or question.

What would you do if you were told at the age of twenty-one you only had one year to live?

SECOND - give your listeners an emotional experience by telling the story of how to overcome the challenge or to find the answer to the opening question.

This is what happened to Professor Stephen Hawking just as he was graduating from Oxford University with a promising career in the Sciences; Professor Hawking seemed to have that bright future taken from him after being diagnosed with a rare form of Motor Neurone Disease. He knew that he had to act fast and started working on his groundbreaking theories... He had to make every day count.

THIRD - galvanise your listeners' response with an eye-opening resolution that calls *them* to action

Professor Hawking despite losing the ability to move and speak independently discovered the Laws of Black Hole Mechanics, Hawking Radiation and wrote the best-seller, "A Brief History In Time." He outlived the doctor's prediction by 60 years and contributed much to the world. If he could do that despite all of his struggles, you are all capable of learning science.

2) Bridging

'Bridging' is a technique where you teach your students new concepts and information by connecting them to something that they already know very well. It's not about making the work easier or harder, which is differentiation. By relating it to things that they have genuine interests in like sports, music or popular culture you are creating an emotional hook that will pull them into your subject.

The key to successful bridging is not to try to align their interests with ours, but for us the teachers, to align our lessons with what they enjoy. This does not mean that we should act like Ali G either: we have to try, without embarrassing ourselves, to discover what naturally interests them and see if there any overlaps with our subjects.

A good example of this was when I was covering a Year 11 English lesson and they were looking at Ted Hughes' poem *Hawk Roosting* and were struggling to connect with the text's themes of power and superiority.

To create a contrast, I gave them a written copy of the lyrics of rapper, Kanye West's "Power" and allowed them to contrast his song with Hughes' prose. Because Kanye West is a popular artist and the students were very familiar with his music, they became very engaged and made many rich contributions to the lesson. With their newfound insights, they could breakdown Hughes' poem a lot more effectively. Bridging must have two main parts:

- WHY - Wherever you can, do not only explain HOW you do something but WHY you do it as well. If students do not see how what they are learning will be useful to them, they will switch off. I once had a NEET cohort that was full of aspiring rappers and singers, but they hated their English lessons. They thought that learning about poetry and Shakespeare was utterly pointless and would not have an impact on their career goals. In response, I told them that all the literary devices that they were learning like metaphors and similes, were crucial for helping them write more interesting songs. Build those connections.
- APPLY - Wherever possible, make sure that your students can take those concepts that they have learnt and can apply it, preferably to a real-world scenario, *as soon as possible*. Maths professor and Education Expert Dr Barbara Oakley states that when learning maths techniques, "you want your brain to become used to the idea that just knowing how to use a particular problem-solving technique isn't enough-you also need to know <u>when</u> to use it[10]." Application aids retention and will make it more likely that your students will engage

THE GOOD

with what they are learning.

3) Enthusiasm

This really goes without saying. You are the emotional climate of the room. If you hate the subject that you teach, this will come through your teaching and your students will hate it too. If they see that you enjoy the subject that you teach, this may rub off on them in the right way.

Have you ever had the experience where your friend wanted you to go to the cinema to watch a film that you were not too keen on? What made you go? Your friend's enthusiasm and persistence finally won you over and you found yourself enjoying the film. Likewise, your students may not be keen on your subject, but your positivity may turn them around. Be like that annoying friend.

4) Healthy Competition

We all like competition — especially when we are winning. Make a game out of some of your lessons like an interactive quiz or a debate. Use the group dynamics to your advantage — in my experience, teenagers like to look 'cool' and one way of doing that is by being better than their peers in something that they all care about. Create a safe and inclusive space where they can let their competitive instincts run riot and watch them learn and have fun doing it.

I remember when I had to cover a Year 11 Citizenship class and we had to talk about the Government Budget and all the things that went it calculating it. I knew that they would turn off as soon as they heard "Government Surplus." So, what I did was I split the class into seven groups that represented different services that we needed like the Armed Forces, Healthcare, Police, the Education sector and so on. In their groups they had to create a presentation, explaining to a "Panel of Experts" why they deserve more money than the other services and then debate each other. It was entertaining and the students learnt a lot about Government Spending too.

Reflection Questions

1. Be totally honest with yourself. Are your lessons boring? Do your students fall asleep or disengage entirely with what you teach? Are you bored with what you teach?
2. In your lessons do you feel you are either doing too much talking or too much writing? Why is that? Depending on the subject, can this be changed?
3. When you set similar topics, do you find that your students groan or protest? Is it the material? Can you change it anyway?

Practical Tips

- With a little practice, the Guber Story Framework can be a potent teaching tool, especially to those students who may be disengaged. Depending on your subject, try to see if you put a couple of stories in there. This could make your classes a lot more lively and enriching.
- If your students talk about a particular subject or topic a lot like the latest game or music, if it is appropriate, learn a little about it and see if you can create a connection with what you are teaching. You may shock your students and win some cool points as well as enhance their education.
- If you are bored in your lesson, chances are that your students are bored too. Change it up. Try to add some more variety. If your students spend a lot of time writing, maybe organise some debates, or vice-versa. This will help keep you and them sane, and stop the subject from getting stale.

Respect the Culture

I love to travel. When I go to a new country, I want to try out the country's cuisine, see the country's most important monuments and try to find out about their history. This is because to understand a country's culture is to understand their people and how to interact with them.

The Oxford Dictionary describes culture as "the ideas, customs, and social behaviour of a particular people or society[11]." People are different. Here in London, England, we live in a very diverse city full of people from different religions, cultures, creeds and world-views. Even if, for argument's sake, where you teach is not outwardly diverse, your students will have experiences and opinions that may be drastically different to yours.

To be a great teacher, you must be aware of the different cultures that influence your learners and know how to navigate and integrate them into your classroom skilfully.

I can imagine some of you rolling your eyes, thinking "Really? How am I going to do this with all the students that I have to teach? I have hundreds of students to plan for." I get it. But trust me if you take the time to try to understand your students' cultural perspectives there are a ton of benefits that can be gained.

- Cultural knowledge – learning and appreciating different cultures in your classroom will give you incredible insights, access and understanding, which can incredibly useful going forward in your career. I once taught in a place called Whitechapel in East London which had a thriving South Asian community, and they made up the bulk of the student body. These students gave me fantastic insights into the different types of religions that the local people practice, the different customs, behaviours and cultural norms that they follow. They even taught me certain words from many of their languages. Although I learnt this several years ago, it has helped me immensely in my teaching career, even to this day.
- Trust - showing cultural sensitivity to your students will help

them trust you, and in turn, they will become more open to your viewpoints. Respect is a two-way street. This creates a space where even if there are differences of opinions, it can be dealt with in a constructive, positive way rather than by fire-fighting (more on that later).

The bottom line is that someone's culture is their identity. Whether its Youth culture, High culture, Popular culture, Asian culture, Afro-Caribbean culture, British culture and everything else, if you do not even try to attempt to understand what is meaningful to your students, then, you will have an uphill struggle in trying to engage them. But how do we as teachers put this into practice? Here are a couple of tips that have helped me.

Say Your Students' Names Correctly and Remember Them

Yes, do this. A person's name is a gateway to their identity. As the child of immigrants myself, I know that when a teacher butchered my name and all my classmates started laughing hysterically at me, it didn't really make me want to like my teacher. If the pronunciation is difficult, ask the student how to say their name and be sure to remember it. Many firefights start because teachers don't take enough time to learn and to say their students' names with respect and dignity.

Dale Carnegie stated, "a person's name to that person is the sweetest and most important sound in any language."[12] I am terrible with names naturally but whenever I enter a new class, I try to make a special effort to learn their names. It's an excellent start.

Be Curious but be Tactful

If your students keep using particular language (which is not offensive or disruptive) ask them what it means. Language is another gateway to culture. If I hear a name that is different from what I know, I will ask the student if their name has a particular meaning and where it originates from. Most students tend to oblige as you are showing that you are open to their background.

THE GOOD

Make it a habit of trying to learn as much about their cultural backgrounds as you possibly can. What you discover can give you a clue into their patterns of behaviour. Obviously, keep this within professional and ethical grounds and don't ask questions, which can be deemed as culturally insensitive. Use a bit of common sense. Imagine you were at a nice dinner party with polite strangers. Now let's take your question: if you would be afraid of asking your newfound acquaintances your query for fear of misunderstanding or cultural insensitivity, then don't ask the student.

Find Common Ground

Despite your differences with your students, more often than not there will be things that you will both enjoy. I am a passionate football fan, and it has always served me well with my students (although being an Arsenal supporter has got me a lot of insults over the years). Being able to have something in common with your students can create a warm atmosphere and you won't lose your authority.

If you can do this well, then you are being 'inclusive' and you are championing diversity in your class. Education specialist Linda Wilson writes "diversity recognises and celebrates differences; it supports equality by respecting rights, valuing individuals' talents and advocating that everyone's skills are fully utilised."[13] This is Teaching 101 right? Now hopefully you have some tools to put into practice.

Reflection Questions

1. Do you work with students who may be culturally different from you? How are they different? Are these differences celebrated or a source of tension?
2. Do you know how many different cultures are represented in your class? How open is your cohort in discussing what is different and what is similar? Have you created a safe space where your students can talk about their similarities and differences freely?
3. How much do you personally know about the cultures in your class? Have you tried to understand these cultures or

have you chosen not to? How do you feel your students would respond if you asked them about their cultural perspectives? If you feel that they would respond negatively, why would that be?

Practical Tips

- Remember everything comes back to the Social Contract. Although you want to be open to different cultural points of view, take a firm stance of views that could be offensive or hurtful to a particular group of people. This will make your classroom emotionally unsafe and will undermine everything you are trying to achieve. You must challenge and confront these statements to educate your students and make sure that the class remains inclusive.
- Be aware that some students may not engage in your lessons because they may feel that you do not understand their culture and their perceptions about how you treat them may show up as disruption. In some cases, your students may not be shy to let you know how they feel in your classroom. If this happens, don't panic. Obviously, always follow the Student Protection and Welfare practices in your organisation. But if it doesn't violate any of your protocols, have an open discussion and sincerely try to understand where they are coming from. Listen with the intent to learn rather than to rebuke. You may learn something that can help you develop a better understanding of your students' background and make your classes run smoother. If this is a persistent problem or you need to dedicate a chunk of time to truly understand their perspectives, contact a member of your Team and arrange to sit with the students in question. See the chapter "Assemble Your Team" for more details.
- Depending on your subject and the curriculum, you may have the flexibility to plan lessons that allow you to celebrate the different types of culture in your class. Maybe you could do a debate around the differences and similarities in culture

or a written piece around their local town or city. Be creative, sensitive and open to learning.

Teach Grit

In this chapter, I want to talk about an F-word. Please do not get offended if I use it. The word I'm talking about is... Failure.

Failure might as well be a swear word in our society. Our society hates failures, no matter the circumstances. When I was growing up, many adults told me that in life "there is absolutely no room for failure." For example, look at most reality talent competitions — we cheer on and worship the near-perfect singers, actors, dancers and entrepreneurs, whereas the ones who are not so good and act a little differently, are laughed at mercilessly, ignoring many of the real issues that they may have in their lives.

Our students often are not immune to these powerful forces in society. Our learners don't want to stand out — being outside the group is the equivalent of death. They, like us, want to be the smartest, the coolest, the most attractive, the most creative and they dare not take a step wrong or face the laughter and 'disrespect' of their peers. No one likes to look stupid, but unfortunately, our educational institutions make it too easy for our students to compare themselves by a grade or a letter and many suffer real problems because they perceive themselves as failures — which can last a lifetime.

When an authority figure like a parent or a teacher labels a young person a failure, it can be especially devastating, causing deep anger, resentment and often severe damage to their budding self-esteem. Christopher "The Notorious BIG" Wallace, considered one of the greatest rappers that ever lived, wrote this on the intro of his mega-hit "Juicy" saying:

"Yeah, this album is dedicated

To all the teachers that told me I'd never amount to nothin'."[14]

Although he was, at this point in his life, a music superstar, multimillionaire and a Hip-Hop icon, what his teachers told him still hurt him enough that he had to shout them out to show them how wrong they were. He was labelled a failure, and now he proved he had got one over them — he succeeded.

THE GOOD

I don't know where you are reading this book from, but in the UK, there is a worrying trend in our country concerning our young students, and I am very confident that these issues affect the young people where you are too.

We have Got Failure All Wrong

At this time of writing, there has been a sharp increase in our young people needing referrals for mental health treatment in the UK. *The Guardian Newspaper* reported that according to figures taken from the National Society for the Prevention of Cruelty to Children (NSPCC), cases in 2018 had "risen by more than a third in the last three years." The article continued that the number of schools seeking professional help was "34,757 in 2017-18, equivalent to 183 every school day. In 2014-15, there were 25,140 referrals."[15]

It doesn't end there either. Teaching magazine *TES* reported on the same issue, questioning how the UK Government's pledge to help tackle this problem will actually help those students in need. *TES* reported, "in numerous charity-led surveys of young people, academic anxiety consistently ranks in the top three reasons for poor mental wellbeing."[16]

In our increasingly busy and pressurised society, our young people are struggling. In our 24/7 world, where our successes and failures can be posted up at the click of a button, our young people's mental and emotional wellbeing has taken a battering.

Why is this important? You, as their teacher, will be at the front line of these experiences. I got my first mobile phone when I was sixteen (I know, I'm a dinosaur) and now we have children as young as three years old holding these devices of mass distraction. If failure was a person, our new digital age has given it steroids and the martial arts skills of Liam Neeson in *Taken*.

Why am I going on about failure? It's simple. When we hear the background stories about the ultra-successful individuals in our society, failure has been a considerable part of their future accomplishments. Failure is a necessary part of learning. In fact, many argue that this is the only way to learn anything of value. Failure means that we are going outside of our comfort zones. Here is a list of the benefits of failure:

- Failure shows us reality — when we try something new, we often have images in our heads that are usually inaccurate. When what we dream doesn't quite go to plan, failure is the mentor that helps us look at what we did wrong, but also what we did right. As a teacher, failure allows us to see precisely how we can support our students get to the next level

- Failure provides invaluable real-world experience —Success is often a one-way street. It's easy to become arrogant when everything goes our way. But that is half the answer: being a success in the classroom is about knowing what to do and what *not to do* and the latter often comes from making mistakes and learning from them.

- Failure grows our character — when we first fail in something, especially if it is something we care about, it can feel like Conner McGregor kicked us in the face. It hurts like hell, and it can feel like the whole world is laughing at us. But if we can recover in a healthy way, we soon realise that failure is separate from who we are as an individual — your failures do not make you any less of a person. I once had a student that flunked an important exam, and she left the classroom distraught and in streams of tears. After I caught up to her, she apologised and was really hard on herself, stating that she felt so "stupid" and "she was the biggest idiot in the class." The irony was that she was academically in the top 5% of the school, so what she said was a massive exaggeration. After I helped her to calm down, I told her that although she didn't do as well as she thought, her poor mark was not a reflection of her as an individual. She had a bad day and that's it — she will bounce back from this result and do better next time. She looked at the parts of the paper that she messed up, smashed the next exam, and she was a lot better for it.

In our classrooms, we have seen this scene played out a thousand times:

1. A student is presented new material to learn

2. The student finds it really difficult
3. The student fools around, avoiding doing the work
4. The student gives up saying "I've never been good at [x] subject" and then spends the whole academic year fooling around in the class.

Sometimes the student messes around because they feel if they never try, they can never fail. Or we have the student that is comfortable with the material but just can't seem to push himself to the next level because he doesn't feel 'good enough' and would rather stay on the plateau — never getting worse but never improving either.

If that sounds like some of the students in your class, you may have to teach them 'grit.'

What is Grit?

Professor Angela Duckworth, a leading expert in Human Resilience, asked the question of what traits separated the top athletes, musicians, entrepreneurs and other leaders in their fields, from the rest of society.

After extensive research, her studies found that it wasn't the people that had inbuilt talent, super confidence or pure genius that often got to the top in their careers - instead, it was the people who *didn't* think that they were anything special and were absolutely determined to get better.

These people were never satisfied with their performance and were always looking for ways to improve. They were disciplined, focused and learnt to cope with the boredom, frustrations and pain that comes with mastering their craft. These high performers trained relentlessly, for months, years and even decades before they achieved the results that they were hoping for.

Despite whatever external rewards came with their developing skills, they were motivated for more intrinsic rewards like mastery and self-actualisation. Duckworth wrote in her book *Grit* "it was this combination of passion and perseverance that made high achievers special."[17]

If you believe that we should be stretching our students to take them to the next level in their education, then they have to learn to reach and sometimes fall short. Failure is a necessary part of their journey, but we don't have to make it a tyrant like the rest of society does. Teaching your students how to be 'gritty' will not only help them in your class but could set them up for life success. Here's a couple of things that you can do to help your students become more gutsy.

Teach Your Students How to Have a Growth Mindset

When it comes to learning new skills and getting better, people often come in two flavours:

The first group believes that our talents and abilities are static and will never change. For example, if you're not good at maths, no matter how much you practice and train, your ability will stay the same. These types of learners have what Carol Dweck calls a 'Fixed Mindset.'

The second group believes that we are born with specific talents and abilities, but they are dynamic and with enough help, training and guidance, they can improve. Dweck would say that this group had a 'Growth Mindset.'

Remember the example I gave above with the student in the classroom? That learner felt that coming out his comfort zone was a waste of time because he "doesn't have it" and he falls further behind becoming a self-fulfilling prophecy.

There are many strategies to help your students cultivate a 'Growth Mindset', and many we have already discussed in this chapter. But a critical point that you must make to your students is that science proves that their abilities are not fixed and they can improve if they are willing to believe that they can.

Dweck writes that talent is not "nature *or* nurture, genes *or* environment. From conception on, there's a constant give and take between the two… Not only do genes and environment cooperate as we develop, but genes *require* input from the environment to work properly[18]." This is the classic 'Hare and Tortoise' stuff — those that have the ability but don't use it, will be in danger of losing to those that are not as naturally talented but work on what they have.

Teach Your Students How To Delay Gratification for Greater Rewards

Pursuing worthy goals like getting good grades, a great career or a great family will have points along the way where it will be tough. There will be times where we all must face boredom, annoyance and pain. But we must teach our students that despite these dark times, we have to dig in and keep on going — there is light at the end of the tunnel.

Let me keep it 100% real with you. Most young people do not understand the importance of time. Teenagers haven't lived enough life to know that our actions, given enough time, will have consequences.

When I was fifteen years of age, the most important things in my life (in no particular order) were football, cartoons, chocolate and girls. If I knew then what I know now, I would have been trading stocks and shares rather than football stickers. Our job as adults is to teach our learners the benefits of giving up a little enjoyment now so they will have a better future later.

When our students feel like this (and this is usually during the exam period or before coursework deadlines), help them to stay motivated. Look at the chapter "Cast a Vision" for lots of tips on how to help your students see a brighter future and continue to affirm your faith in them. When they feel that the tasks that are doing are tedious, give them plenty of breaks and perhaps show them lots of motivational videos about people whom they admire but had to work hard to get to where they wanted to be.

Allow times where they can talk to you and others in their class about how their feelings and frustrations about the work they are doing. By giving your students healthy outlets, they will feel that they are being listened to and that they are ultimately not alone.

Teach Your Students the 'Slight Edge'

This concept has literally changed my life and it came from one of the greatest personal development books I have ever read. 'The Slight Edge' was written by entrepreneur Jeff Olsen and details many things that he learnt on his way to being a multi-millionaire.

So, what is The Slight Edge? This concept is straightforward: There is an invisible force that is evoked with every single decision we make, good or bad, big or small. This force is never neutral, so if we always make lots of good choices daily like eating healthy foods, saving and investing our money and spending quality time with loved ones then eventually this will lead us to wealth, happiness, love and success in our lives.

But if we make lots of minor errors in our daily routines, like bingeing on fast food, spending more than we earn, not improving our skills and not cultivating positive relationships, given enough time, this will snowball into financial meltdown, poor health and general misery.

We live in a fast world, and we now take for granted the speed in which we can make good outcomes occur. We live in a society that believes in instant gratification — reality shows can take ordinary people and within a few weeks, make them rich and famous. Instead of going to the library to find new information, we have all the world's knowledge at our fingertips through our smartphones. We have near-instant communication where we can video-chat with someone on the other side of the planet with little delay, so it's no wonder that our students now think that getting educated should be instant too!

The Slight Edge's message is crystal clear: small, measurable and consistent steps lead to tremendous results, and this is something that I drill into all the students that I teach. The problem with humans, in general, is that we are so focused on seeing the massive results that we feel that our small actions are utterly insignificant. But when we look at our choices over weeks, months, years and decades, only then do we have the foresight to see where our habits and decisions lead us to. Please do not sell this to your students as the Magic Bullet to success - the Slight Edge requires work and patience and your students will need to know that from the get-go. Olsen said, "the path of success is inconvenient, and therefore not just easy not to do but *easier* not to do. For most people, it's easier to stay in bed. Getting on the path and staying on the path requires faith in the process."[19]

I once had a Year 11 student that struggled to read books because he felt that he didn't have time to read anything. I challenged him and said that if he read for a mere fifteen minutes a day — which was how long his bus ride home would take, that within a year, he could read eight novels.

He didn't believe me, so I broke down the maths to him: Let's say we take out all the major breaks like Christmas, Easter and Bank Holidays and out of a 365 day year, he reads for only 320 days. Also, let's assume the average novel is around 400 pages long and has 300 words a page. The average adult reads about 250-300 words per minute but because he wasn't a confident reader, he could only read 200 words a minute. Here's how we got that eight novel figure:

- 400 pages x 300 words = 120,000 words in the whole book.
- 120,000 words in the whole book/200 words he reads per minute = 600 minutes to read the entire thing
- 600 minutes to read the entire book/60 minutes = 10 hours to read an average novel
- 15 minutes a day x 320 days = 4800 minutes of reading in the whole year excluding holidays
- 4800 minutes/60 minutes = 80 hours of reading in the year
- So, 80 hours of reading in the year/10 hours it takes to read an average novel = 8 novels in the year

The little habit of reading on his way back from school could produce that significant result at the end of the year. Tell your students that every single decision that they make matters and it will bear fruit one day. If they are struggling with a particular task, ask them to break it done into tiny, doable chunks. Teach them to be tortoises, not hares.

Reflection Questions

1. Do you have students that often complain that the tasks you set are too hard and they won't engage? What strategies have you put in place to help them? What has worked and what hasn't?
2. In general, do you have students that seem to give up when the work gets difficult and they procrastinate? Do they disrupt the class? If this happens, how do you deal with this disruption? Do you sanction their behaviour or do you listen?
3. Do you have students who are perfectionists? Do they only attempt the easy tasks and avoid doing the harder ones? What strategies do you use to deal with them and have they worked?

Practical Tips

- I would highly recommend buying these two books: *Mindset* by Dr Carol Dweck and *The Slight Edge* by Jeff Olson. My extremely brief summaries of their core ideas do not do their books justice. In both books, there are tons of strategies from how to praise effectively, how to teach your students new material and many tactics to help you keep your students happy and motivated. They are an absolute must-have on any teacher's bookshelf.
- Make your class "failure-friendly." In my classes, I often say to my students "I don't mind if you fail, but I will mind if you don't try." Drill into your students that 'failure is never final' and that if they try and they fail, it was an event, not a destiny. Celebrate effort as much as successful results, especially for students who may not be as strong in your subject. This is about making your students more resilient and willing to keep on going.
- As always, with this chapter, sprinkle a very healthy dose of common sense. Some students may feel that they can do

whatever they want and not bother. If they are applying absolutely no effort and they have a bad attitude towards you or the tasks at hand, you may have to use the strategies listed in the "Bad" and "Ugly" sections of this book.

Tell Your Story

One of my favourite teaching heroes is a chap called Socrates. His CV is impressive: being seen as the Father of Modern Philosophy, teacher to some of the greatest thinkers that ever existed such as Xenophon and of course Plato and even captained the 1982 Brazil Football Team… oh sorry, wrong Socrates. OK apart from the last one, Socrates' ideas still have clout today.

What I found personally fascinating were his views on learning. He believed that as human beings, true education was knowledge of self and should not only make you smarter but make you a better human being — which he described as being virtuous. Writer Peter Kreeft neatly sums up Socrates philosophy stating "you can be *knowledgeable* without knowing yourself, but you cannot be *wise* without knowing yourself[20]." Socrates once stated that "the unexamined life is not worth living" and that statement has always reminded me to be more conscious and deliberate in my everyday actions.

In our technologically advanced age, where jobs are getting automated and as we edge closer to a world resembling *The Matrix*, there is one thing that a robot can never do — know what it's like to be human.

The Internet and the 'machines' can never replicate your experiences and wisdom. For all the reasons that we have mentioned in the previous chapters, you are more than an android. You do more than just spout facts, figures and data. You are a human being with experiences that are unique to you and can hold invaluable information for your students.

There is a Chinese proverb "before you go on a long journey, talk to the person who has just come back." Despite all the books our students read and all the qualifications that they get, nothing beats life experience and yours could be the key to unlocking your students' potential.

Your Story Can Make You Inspirational to Your Students

My NEET students taught me this lesson. I was raised in a rough part of East London and when my students told me many of the stories, I could empathise with their situations. I would often explain to them that despite the area that I grew up in, I managed to find a way out through education. I am now in a position to help my family, make good money and don't have to look over my shoulder every time I leave the house. If I could do that, then they can easily do it too.

Unfortunately, many of the guys that I grew up with, walked down a terrible path into drugs, prison and stagnation and I often told my students that it could also happen to them if they didn't change. These stories gave my pupils reference points and an opportunity to learn from the mistakes of those who already walked in their shoes.

Your Story Can Make You Relatable

The fact that you are willing to share some of your experiences shows that you can empathise with your students and that they can do so in turn. This is great for helping you and your students climb up Trust Mountain together and create a more harmonious classroom. Your stories could validate their own experiences and provide positive solutions that they may never have considered on their own.

Your Story Can Help Your Students Tell Their Own

I once had a student who I will call 'Derek' who had severe ADHD and had a mild form of Autism. Derek had a tough life before he came to our special Outreach programme. Derek and his sister were adopted at a very young age and they were shunted around different foster homes, but because of his unique challenges, he didn't tend to stay in one place very long. Derek fell in with the wrong friends and started to act up in school and ended up getting kicked out and was placed in our course. Derek was at first disruptive, hyper and needed constant supervision. He was a nightmare to teach and at first, we struggled.

But although Derek may have been difficult to deal with, he was incredibly perceptive and self-aware and after we managed to crack his tough shell, he revealed his anger, frustration and extremely low self-esteem. Derek thought that he was worthless because his parents abandoned him and he bought into that belief. It was heartbreaking to hear his story. Over my time working with him, I shared my story about the difficulties that I had in school with my behaviour and how I struggled for many years. But through hard work, great teachers and mentors, I slowly turned things around. As time went on, Derek started to become more responsive and positive in class. Working with his Learning Support Assistant, he began to shake that negative label that he had over himself and he started to improve academically.

At the end of the term, we had a talent showcase where we invited parents, relatives, local celebrities and anyone we could get through the doors to see the talents of our superstars. Derek decided to perform a rap song detailing the struggles in his life and his hopes for the future and he absolutely smashed his set. For us, this was a very proud moment, Derek was leaving but he had done a complete turnaround in terms of his behaviour and he was the star attraction.

After he had done his rap, Derek made an impromptu speech, speaking about his challenges but also all the support he had received, and saying that he is applying for university because he now believed in himself. Most of the staff, including me, were in tears because of how far Derek had come. Derek went to study at university, completing a Business Administration degree, passing with flying colours. Never underestimate the power of your story — it could literally save someone's life.

THE GOOD

Story Ideas

Of course, every single situation is unique. Your learners are at different points of Trust Mountain and all these factors will need to be considered. Here's a couple of tips that you can use to help you draw out your own stories.

- Use cultural knowledge - In the subject that you are teaching, your cultural background - for example your race, religion or nationality - may give unique insights that may help you enhance your lessons. Your experiences take your subject from a black and white textbook to a real, human experience that your students can truly engage with. I once observed a German History teacher talking about how her great grandfather had fought for the Nazis during World War II. She spoke about her family's experiences after the Allies won and the severe repercussions that it carried for her clan. We were transfixed when she told us the stories that were passed down by her grandparents, parents, uncles and aunts and humanised the devastating conflict. Nobody in the room spoke or interrupted as she counted the human cost of this legacy and how she saw herself as a German. It was a compelling lesson that had me on the edge of my seat — you have more stories than you think.
- Use local knowledge - if you happen to be from the same area where you are teaching in, this information can prove invaluable as you may be able to understand the local lingo, slang and conventions that are not known to outsiders. As I have taught mainly in London for the majority of my career, being from the East End has served me really well as I understand the codes, attitudes and mindsets that my students present in class. This local knowledge helps me teach my students in a way that they can understand and access.
- Use professional experience - if you worked in an industry before you became a teacher, it's always great to have a

couple of stories showing how you used your knowledge in the real world. I know a Geography teacher who was a chartered surveyor in a previous career. He had intimate knowledge of when, why and how certain buildings, roads and infrastructure were set up and that helped bring his subject to life. He was also a great mentor to the students who wanted to become surveyors themselves giving them the inside knowledge of the profession.

But there is one thing that I must warn you about when using this strategy. Always, always, always follow the rules and regulations of your particular institution. These rules are there to protect you. Do not give any information that is compromising, not age appropriate or unprofessional.

There is such as a thing as oversharing: talking about things that are deeply private or personal will make you lose authority, open to abuse, cost your job and, if it's dire, get you in trouble with the law. As always, maintain your boundaries and use the Line Manager Test: if you were going to say something in class that your Line Manager would not be pleased about, then don't say it to your students. Keep it classy.

Reflection Questions

1. Reflecting on yourself, your students and your subject knowledge are there any anecdotes that could help you in the classroom? Do you use them? If not, why not?
2. Do you share any common ground with your students? Do you have cultural, local or professional knowledge? How can you use it to help you teach?
3. Have you ever struggled when you were in school/college/university? How did you overcome those challenges? Could you make this experience into a story to motivate your students?

Practical Tips

- If you have any students who are consistently demotivated and you can connect with them through cultural, local or professional knowledge, try to see if maybe five minutes before or after the lesson, you have a quick chat with them offering your wisdom and support. It has to be organic: if you have a student who is adversarial, this may backfire. Build a bit of a relationship with them first, then try.
- It's always good to have a good couple of stories to hand. Go through your experiences both academically or professionally. Have you got stories that are interesting? Inspirational? Tragic? Funny? Remember these stories and where appropriate try them with your students. Remember the Line Manager Test and your professional boundaries - do not overshare as it could cost you dearly.
- Keep your stories preferably short and sweet. Unless you are a master storyteller, a half an hour story may bore the life out of your students and it will defeat the purpose of the exercise. If you are utterly clueless about what to say, go back to the Chapter "Don't Be Boring" and look at the tips there.

The Bad

Positives, Compliants & Disrupters

Right at the beginning of the book, I introduced you to the "Trust Mountain" theory. In this chapter, I want to look in greater detail how these different student types mix in the classroom.

For you to really understand this chapter, I have to introduce you to a concept called the "Pareto Principle" which is also called the "80/20 Rule." This rule was named after the 19th Century Italian economist Vilfredo Pareto and was based on his work on uneven wealth distribution amongst the populations in Western Europe. To put it simply, Pareto came up with a startling discovery which was:

- 80% of the country's wealth was held by only 20% of the country's population.

Pareto studied other Western countries and saw that this pattern was remarkably similar across the board. His studies are what gave birth to his legendary rule.

According to Wikipedia, the "Pareto Principle" states that "for many events, roughly 80% of the effects come from 20% of the causes[1]." Sounds complicated doesn't it? Let's use some real-world examples to clear this up. Legend has it that Pareto loved gardening and being the clever clogs that he was, would track the yields that his fruits and veg gave him. When looking at his peas, Pareto discovered that:

- 80% of his peas only came from 20% of the pods.

Other examples of Pareto's Law include:

- 80% of the goals scored in football (or soccer) come from 20% of the players
- In a company, 80% of sales are made by 20% of the salespeople
- 80% of the electricity in your home is used by only 20% of the appliances
- 80% of your results will be achieved by doing only 20% of your tasks and so on.

It doesn't have to be *exactly* 80/20. If you look at different instances across different events, it could be 70/30 or 90/10 or even 99/1, but the fact remains there is an unequal balance. So how does that relate to teaching, I hear you ask? Good question. In my several years of teaching and observing my peers, I have noticed that:

- 80% of your behaviour management issues will come from 20% of your students.

Before I go on, I really want to hammer home a very, very important point.

Remember when I am using this theory I am talking about the STUDENT'S BEHAVIOUR and not the STUDENT'S CHARACTER. No matter how terrible, your students are, this chapter is not giving you an excuse to organise a witch-hunt.

Please underline that line. Going back to the "Student Triangle," if we do have a student that misbehaves in the class, unless we have a full understanding of who they are, the environment that they have come from and how they feel about their school life, it will be incredibly unfair to make a permanent judgement of their character.

Most disruptive behaviour is often a symptom of something going on in another part of their life. Also, it could be your student's relationship with the subject — your student could absolutely love Chemistry but hate Drama and by proxy, transfer their frustrations onto you.

Remember in our everyday lives we can play many different roles that bring out different sides of us. For example, an elite heavyweight boxer may have to be aggressive and brutal in the boxing ring, but at home with his family, he is kind, compassionate and caring — does that mean he is two different people? Likewise, different subjects, situations and teachers could bring out different sides to our students. Our job is to create a space, where we can get the best out of our learners and give them the chance to shine.

This theory looks at whether particular students show the same patterns of behaviour over a fixed period and having that awareness, allows us to change our game plan. For this chapter, I will leave out our Engaged learners (Level Four) as they cause no behaviour issues so we will talk about the other three levels: Positives, Complaints and

THE BAD

Disrupters. I have also flipped the triangle to show how these students are distributed. You will see what I mean in the next couple of pages.

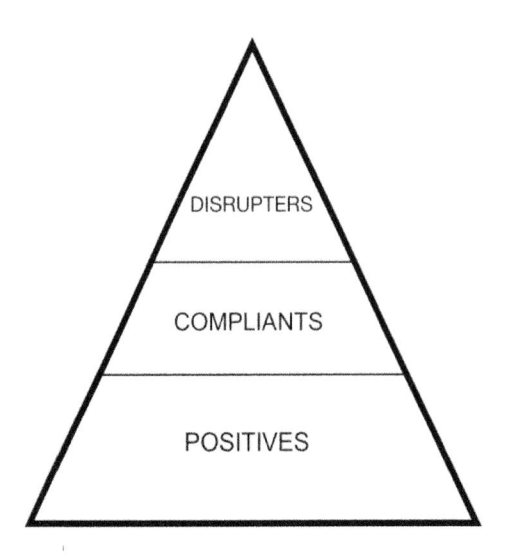

```
         /\
        /  \
       /DISRUPTERS\
      /------------\
     /  COMPLIANTS  \
    /----------------\
   /    POSITIVES     \
  /_____\
```

I want you to imagine a class full of thirty students. The exact numbers may vary but in general, the students will fall into three categories in terms of their typical behaviour. If you are already teaching, imagine a class that you have some difficulties with and see how they stack up next to these descriptions.

POSITIVES - These guys usually take up the majority of the class. These students tend to be pleasant, want to get on with their work and will do as asked without arguments. Depending on their age, other students may distract them, but they tend to settle quickly, show a lot more initiative and can direct themselves. In this example, combined with the Engaged learners, they should at least number twenty-three members of the class.

COMPLIANTS - These guys are also known as 'fencers' because in terms of behaviour, they do just that — they sit on the fence between Positives and Disrupters and depending on how they are managed can fall on either side.

Compliants tend to be more prone to distraction and these are the students that you will constantly ask to follow your instructions.

"Compliants" specialise in low-level disruption, talking, wasting time, irritating others and these are the guys that end up being moved to another part of the classroom (depending on their age).

Compliants tend to heed warnings and temporarily stop their disruptive activities, but these are the guys that you have to watch and micromanage to stay on task. Sometimes one or two warnings may do the trick and as the lesson goes on, with any luck, they may settle.

This area is where you will tend to find the 'standup comedians' or 'pranksters' and these guys like to have the last word. More often than not, you will find that Compliants will take their cues from the Disrupter or the other 'leaders' in the room. In a class of thirty, you may get four or five that fit this description.

DISRUPTERS - They are the Bad Boys and Bad Girls of your institution. These students are the ones who consistently come late to your lessons, are very reluctant to do any work and will not engage with you in any positive way.

The main difference between a Complaint and a Disrupter is the way that they respond to authority and how quickly the situation can become a flashpoint. In general, a Complaint may settle down after you speak to them about their behaviour, but a Disrupter will often ignore or at the more extreme end, become confrontational or aggressive, forcing you into a "firefight" (I'll talk about that later). These students are often sent out of class and will receive the bulk of sanctions.

If you are really unlucky you may get what I call a "Passive Disrupter" - these students are absolute masters of passive aggression and stealth tactics. These wiseguys are the types who will tend to pretend that you are not there and will follow your instructions but in a way that causes absolute havoc to your class.

A classic example I had was with a Year 10 student - I will call "Zack" - who would take absolutely forever to do anything that I asked him to do, and when my back was turned, would aggravate other students. When I would challenge him on his behaviour, he would kick off saying "I'm doing the work! What's your problem?" Charming, I know. If I asked him to move to another seat, Zack would make sure that he barged everyone on the way there. Once he got sanctioned, he would usually explode as he felt that the everyone in the class was trying to "set him up" which would lead to another flashpoint. These guys are maddening because they make themselves out to be the victim rather than you, the poor teacher who is losing hair daily because of them.

In general, a Disrupter is often the "alpha" of the space encouraging the Compliants to play-up and shutting down students and teachers alike who try to stop their bad behaviour. Disrupters are very aware of their reputations, and some may use it to try to get their own way often saying things like "I don't do any work anyway" or "the other teachers let me do what I want so why can't you?"

These students often are the most challenging to deal with and in a classroom of thirty, maybe one or two will fit this description.

If you combine your Compliants and Disrupters together, in our class of thirty students, six or seven students could potentially take up 80% of your time when dealing with behaviour — a sobering thought.

Remarkably, when I did my NEETs work with learners who were kicked out of school, members of gangs and generally very disillusioned with education, they would still fall into these three categories. Although the NEET classes were a lot smaller (fourteen students or less), I found the exact same issues that I found in most primary and secondary schools and I had to devise strategies that addressed each category.

If you are a normal human being, there is a part of you that may be thinking, "Why don't I kick out all the Disrupters? According to your theory, my lessons should be 'smooth sailing.' Not necessarily chum.

As with most things in life it is not as simple as that. Here are a few things to consider:

You Could Do More Damage in the Long Term

In the short term you may get a little more peace in your classroom, but in the long term this may come back to haunt you. Depending on the organisation that you work in, you may not be able to kick them out of your class so easily. Usually, there will have to be a process, so unless they have done something horrifying, you will have to deal with them for a while. In the meantime, these students tend to respond very poorly if they feel that you are victimising them. This will cause even more disruption as they will think that they have to get 'their vengeance' and you will find yourself in the next couple of weeks, months and years in an epic battle every time you meet that individual. This is something that you don't want to deal with along with everything else in your workday.

You May Not be able to Avoid the Student

Even if you get the student removed from your class, depending on the institution that you teach in, you may not be able to avoid that student. Again, because the relationship is very hostile, this student may egg on his or her friends to carry on their cause in your absence and further undermine your authority. I kid you not, I have seen Disrupters that have been kicked out of the class, organise campaigns with their remaining peers to terrorise their teacher. Also, if you have to speak to this student in and around your institution, such as in the canteen, the playground or on a school trip, the chances will increase that you will end up in a firefight which will make yours and everyone else's life extremely difficult.

We Have a Duty of Care and They Deserve a Chance

Trust me, I know how it feels when you have an extremely challenging student. I am not suggesting that we "hug all their cares away" or give them milk and cookies and a friendly pat on the head. If these students are behaving in a way that is extremely inappropriate or abusive, then I would be the first to tell you not to tolerate that behaviour and it needs to be sanctioned.

From my own personal experience dealing with some of the most troubled and disaffected students in London, once you heard some of their stories, you will understand why they are the way that they are.

Sometimes these students do not understand why they behave in that way themselves, and sometimes my colleagues and I were the only positive authority figures in their lives. I have taught students whose parents have been murdered, committed suicide, become severe drug addicts, come from all types of severe dysfunction and had emotional and physical traumas that I still cannot completely understand. But although they have gone through so much difficulty, they have survived and they could have a bright future — one that you can help shape.

I know that there are students that have had a decent life and with no major trauma, but they still want to play up — go figure. But… always remember, their behaviour is a symptom of something more profound and they may need our help.

This theory is relevant because it helps you see where the potential behaviour management issues will come from and allows you to prepare a plan to deal with them as they arise.

Your ability to manage behaviour depends on your ability to understand your students and come up with the right strategies at the right time. Especially with Disrupters, one wrong step will totally derail your whole lesson.

In my experience, the key to turning around a Disrupter is the strength of your relationship — you will need to walk the tightrope between being empathetic and a listening ear, but also being able to create healthy boundaries and be ready to enforce them when needed. It's tough but totally doable — especially when you take an interest and try to see the good in them — even it is as small as a teaspoon of water.

Become a Detective

Your job is straightforward: You are now to become a detective and observe all the patterns that you see when your students enter your classroom. All the great teachers that I have seen, know their students' personalities, traits and quirks and can tailor their approach to each pupil. Remember do not make a snap judgement – observe your students' patterns over a significant amount of time. If they have bad days, take mental notes on anything that could have been the cause like the weather, the time of year, friends or outside issues. All the information that you gather will make you more effective at preventing and stopping disruptive behaviour in the future. Know your class and know your students and you can win 1000 firefights.

Reflection Questions

1. Think of a class you have taught that didn't go well. What were the ratios of Positives, Compliants and Disrupters? How much do you know about the Compliants and Disrupters? Have you built a relationship with them?
2. What are the Compliants and Disrupters they like in other classes? Are the same or are they different? If they are why — can you find any clues?
3. Look at the dynamics of your class? Who do the Disrupters and Compliants sit next to? Do they change when one of their peers is absent? How so?

Practical Tips

- In the "Ugly" section, in the chapter "Build Your Team," I go into detail on how to get external support dealing with individual students, but, for now, ask other teachers in your department and beyond about the students who are disruptive. Try to compare notes and look at how they deal with their behaviour. Even if they are disruptive with other teachers, in a weird way, this may be a relief because you know you are not the only one who is struggling, and you can bounce ideas off your colleagues that may help you learn how to deal with them. Even better still, if you find a teacher that has a positive relationship with the Disrupter, grill them and take notes: ask them for any advice, tips, tricks and strategies that they use and try them in the next lesson. Learn

THE BAD

> all their secrets as if your class depends on it — because it does.

- Also, in the "Ugly" section, in the chapter "Interventions and Letting Go," I discuss how to have assertive conversations with tricky students, but here it may be worth pulling one or two of the more disruptive learners aside and asking them how to make your relationship positive. If they are not completely hostile towards you, ask to have a chat after the lesson and tell them that they are not in any trouble at all — that's important! In this case, this could be a more mellow conversation where you are genuinely trying to figure them out. Use "The Student Triangle", obviously with tact and appropriateness, to see if you could figure out what makes your student tick and see if you can find common ground. Look at the chapter "Respect the Culture" for tips on how to do this.

- Experiment with where the individuals are seated. If you have a high concentration of Disrupters and Compliants sitting together then perhaps moving them to different parts of the class, may help stop the disruption. If you find that your class is full of too many Compliants and Disrupters, talk to your Head of Department or colleagues to see if you could swap some students out to create a more mellow balance.

Be Just, Fair and Firm

Consistency and Boundaries

If you want to maintain the respect of your students, you absolutely must be consistent when it comes to classroom management. I was once told that the English Oak Tree could live for up 200 years. The trees that tended to survive the longest may not be biggest or the tallest but are the trees that can combine strength, durability and flexibility. When the big storms hit, these flexible trees sway with the wind rather than try to stand tall and get blown over. With your behaviour management strategy, you must be able to stand firm in your decisions but have some flexibility and creativity.

The Social Contract is the law of the land that you and your class agreed to as a community, and your responsibility is to uphold those ideals. If you can do this successfully, you will build a reputation as someone who is likeable but also someone who is tough on the things that matter.

Most of the issues that you will face in class will be about boundaries — and what happens when people cross them. We all have boundaries: boundaries at work, emotional boundaries, physical boundaries and so on. If we didn't have strong, healthy boundaries, our lives would be utter chaos. Cloud and Townsend wrote "boundaries are anything that helps you differentiate from someone else or show where you begin and you end." [2]

Good fences make for good neighbours. As much as you may love your neighbours, you wouldn't appreciate them walking in your house in the middle of the night uninvited. That would be a violation of your boundaries and I'm sure like me, you would eventually reach for the telephone to call the police, or worse. Your students have to understand that everyone has a responsibility to manage their own boundaries and not cross other peoples. If they do, they must be encouraged to do what they can to make it right.

Just as we have different laws and different consequences when they are broken, your class will need a clear warning system and sanctions for when the Social Contract is broken. There are loads of factors that will determine how you set up your own system, but I would advise that you to follow the procedures that have been set up by the institution but always tie it to the Social Contract you established in your class. Here are a couple of strategies to use to keep your classes as sweet as a nut.

Always Go Back to The Contract

Whenever someone is being disruptive, show the student where they are going wrong based on what you agreed. Sometimes this may not have to be verbal — pointing or tapping the Social Contract could be enough to stop any minor breaches from your pupils.

But if you have a student who is persistently breaching the agreement, when you are not busy, speak to the culprit at their desk or have a quick two-minute conversation outside the classroom. State clearly what rule they have broken and end it with an open question. For example, you could state "we agreed to respect and listen each other when we speak, and I felt like you weren't doing that. Do you feel the same way?" This gives the student the chance to reflect on their own behaviour and helps you understand their emotional state.

Using open-ended questions allows you to enquire rather than accuse — you don't want to start a firefight and you don't want your learner to feel that you are cornering them. Honestly, if the incident is minor and your class is not going crazy in your absence, try to give the student time to reply. Most Engaged and Positive students can state how they felt, see your point of view, look at what went wrong and be able to self-correct. But if you have a student who has been emotionally hijacked, irritated, or continues to be defiant, then use the next step.

The Easy Road or The Hard Road

If, after you have had a polite conversation with the learner, they continue to disrupt the classroom, bar it being a major incident like fighting or verbal abuse, then I suggest you use "The Easy Road or The Hard Road."

Where possible, try to talk to the student privately and calmly — the disruption could disturb other students or other classes and the learner in question may feel that you are trying to embarrass them, which could make communication difficult. Once you have created that space to talk, you present your student with two options based on what happened in the class. One is the Easy Road - this is an opportunity to resolve the situation whether it is an apology, following the procedure or correcting what went wrong. The other choice is the Hard Road, which will involve a consequence and a possible sanction. Here is an example:

"Justin, we agreed at the beginning of term that we were going to listen and respect each other, but you have been quite rude to me and your classmates. I spoke to you earlier about this and you told me that you would stop but now you upset Richie who was getting on with his work. Now you have to pick a road: The Easy Road would be apologising to Richie getting on with the work that you were meant to, quickly, until the end of the lesson. If you cannot do that, then you have chosen The Hard Road which would mean that you will force me to give you a twenty-minute detention and call your parents. I will give you a minute to make your decision."

The key to this strategy is choice. You have put the ball in the student's court. In doing this, you are asking your student to take responsibility for their behaviour while giving them an opportunity to pick a response.

Another reason why this is effective is because you are giving the student a minute or two to calm down and come out of being 'emotionally hijacked' (see the chapter 'Beware of the Emotional hijack'). After the time period that you set, come back and ask for their answer. If they don't answer, then they have chosen The Hard Road and then you must follow through with whatever sanction or procedures that you have in place.

Benefits Not Features

While I was studying at university, I worked in Central London as a high-end furniture salesperson. At the time, foolishly, I looked at the job as something that helped me pay for my books, my parties and my very healthy diet of Pizza Hut Pepperoni Supremes and Lucozades, and I didn't respect the craft of sales. At this store, all shop-floor salespeople had to complete a training course on Customer Service and Salesmanship. Although I have forgotten most of what was in the module, something was branded on my young mind and has been with me ever since: "Sell Benefits, Never Features."

The thinking went like this: when our customers stepped through the doors of our store, they are coming in to satisfy a need such as buying a new leather sofa or a single bed. We were taught the reason why most customers hated salespeople was, most of the time, the salesperson wasn't interested in the customer's needs. A lousy salesperson wants to flog whatever stuff they had available to hit their sales target leaving the customer feeling like they weren't being listened to. Have you ever tried to buy a car from a dodgy car showroom? Then you have met this type of sales professional.

On the other hand, a great salesperson was like an excellent waiter in a posh restaurant. Great waiters enhance the diner's experience by listening, advising and making sure that they get the best meal that will suit their tastes. The great salespeople are detectives who investigate what the customer needs, why they need it and try to match the customer's need with the best product that they had available.

Here's the kicker: Once the salesperson identified the product that could solve that problem, rather than talk about what the product does (features) she would talk about how the product would specifically help her fulfil his needs (benefits). So, here's an example using that brown leather sofa for a busy father of two young children, who was concerned about how to keep it clean.

"The sofa comes with full grain French leather as standard." This is a feature sales pitch.

"This sofa has the highest quality leather which is easy to clean, hard to stain and can stand up to anything that your two little bundles of joy can throw at it. If any spills do occur, you can use a warm damp cloth to wipe it down and it should be as good as new." This statement is a benefits pitch. It has identified the user's needs and came up with possible solutions if the kids go wild with their hand paints.

The first statement appealed to the father's logic, but the second statement appealed to his wants and guess what? Human beings tend to have a lot of wants.

You are a salesperson too. As a teacher, you are selling your students on the idea that you are worth being listened to. When you are dealing with your students either positively or negatively, never sell features. Most teachers try to appeal to them purely using logic when we should be trying to appeal to them from their interests. Going back to that example where the student has repeatedly broken the Social Contract, you could say:

"If this behaviour continues, I will be forced give you a twenty-minute detention." This doesn't sound like an inconvenience and this will make them more likely to continue. Let's try it again from another angle.

"If this behaviour continues, I will be forced to keep you back for twenty minutes on Friday afternoon which means that will be late for football practice and may not be able to play in the match." Which one sounds more compelling? Just like when you "cast a vision,", paint a picture for where certain negative behaviours will lead them and walk them through how to avoid those consequences.

Address the Behaviour, Not the Person

When addressing your students, no matter how persistent the behaviour that they display, always address the behaviour and not the person. The next couple of tips have helped me in my quest.

Avoid Speaking in Absolutes

"You are always talking in my class"

"You are never on time"

"Every day I have call home to speak to one of your parents"

Always, never, every day. There's not much wriggle room is there? Even if your students are continuing to show repeated patterns of bad behaviour, by saying this to them, you are conveying that this is something that they may never be able to change. The fastest way get someone's back up is to start the statement with "you." Wherever you can, try using "I" instead.

Let's revisit the statements above and transform them using our 'I' message.

"I feel that you may be getting a little distracted by others in the classroom — what's going on?"

"I think that maybe we need to review your timekeeping for registration."

"I am concerned about the behaviour that you have been displaying in some of your other classes and this causes me to get your parents involved. What can we do to turn this situation around?"

Addressing their behaviour starting with "I" allows you to express your viewpoint non-aggressively and is a lot more collaborative. Talking about your own thoughts and feelings invites your learner to the same. Remember, this is not an opportunity to fight fire with fire, but to try to build a relationship. Also, this forces you to deliberate on the words that you are about to say and can help calm the situation down when you are 'emotionally hijacked' — that will be explained later.

Reflection Questions

1. Have you felt that you have been inconsistent in your approach to classroom management? Why do you think that has been the case? Does this differ from class to class and why?
2. If a student repeatedly breaks the rules in your classroom, how do you respond? When speaking about their behaviour, do you do this privately or in front of their other peers? If you have tried both ways, have you seen a difference?
3. When you have to sanction behaviour, what is your typical approach? Do you issue an order, or do you give your learners a choice in how to go forward? Do you walk your students through the consequences of their actions?

Practical Tips

- Consistency, consistency, consistency. Whatever rules you set, you absolutely MUST stick to them, especially in the early days. If you don't keep to what you set up, then you will potentially lose the trust and respect of your students. Have the Social Contract on display and, if necessary, remind your students orally what these rules mean.

- This is a process, and if enforcing the Social Contract is difficult and the students don't respond well, don't lose heart. Always remind yourself that you are working for the good of everyone in the classroom including those who may not comply. Compliants and Disrupters will to test the boundaries with you repeatedly, especially if you are a new teacher. For students who are not used to following any rules, this will be a shock to the system and sometimes they may even behave *worse* than normal to test your mettle. Stand firm and sanction where necessary. Take it class by class. If you still feel unconfident in giving sanctions, go to the "Ugly" section and read the chapter "Sanction Quickly Then Restore."

- Of course, use lots of emotional intelligence when dealing with your students and you may have to vary your approaches depending on the situation. I am not saying that you must appeal to their wants all the time. There are times where you will need to get them engaged logically, but this is where your knowledge of your students comes in. If you are stuck, consult your Team.

Set Milestones

The longer you teach, the more likely you will come across students who will not do any work at all. Surprisingly it's not just the Disrupters or the Compliants, it could also be Positives as well (see chapter "Positives, Complaints & Disrupters.") This can be really frustrating, and sometimes it feels like you are dragging a dead horse up a hill. The automatic assumption could be that they are just being difficult, but there could be other issues at play. Here are a couple of reasons to consider.

1. The Work Is Too Hard

This is usually the first port of call. If you have a student that regularly has this problem, then it may be good just to check whether you have adequately differentiated the work to suit their needs.

If this occurs regularly, your student can become disillusioned and will start slipping further and further down the Trust Mountain. Their frustrations may begin to boil over into increased disruption in your classroom. If you come across this situation often, this must be flagged up and dealt with.

2. The Work Is Too Easy

Surprisingly, this issue can come up too. Students, especially those who excel in your subject, may look at the work as beneath their current ability and may mess around out of boredom. This type of student may do things like try to hurry you along until they get to the part that interests them, disrupt the class by calling out, or disengaging from the lesson entirely. From my experience, this usually comes from three sources: Perfectionism, the Dunning-Kruger Effect or simply the Fear of Failure.

Perfectionism

Students that tend to excel in your subject can be afflicted by the need to be perfect all the time. These types of learners have abilities that are well recognised by everyone and can very competitive, pushing themselves to stay at the top of the class. The downside is that they often can be very critical of themselves and others and create a negative atmosphere in their group. They can also be very impatient and may disregard the work that you set them as 'too easy' ignoring you or their teammates, causing tension and conflict.

The Dunning-Kruger Effect

Wikipedia describes the Dunning-Kruger Effect as "a cognitive bias in which people of low ability have illusory superiority and mistakenly assess their cognitive ability as greater than it is."[4] In other words, they feel that they are the elite when they are really average or below par. Dunning-Kruger students do not have the reflection skills to be able to recognise that their ability does not match up with the superstar status that they have built up in their heads. Think about any reality singing show competitions where the singers boast about their amazing vocals only sound like a cat that is being strangled while thrown off a high-rise building.

From my own personal experience, these students are often self-taught, having a rough idea of how to perform the skill but not knowing the finer details. Further down the line, their arrogance stops them from learning and at the more difficult levels, can come unstuck.

The Fear of Failure

Lastly, students who fail to do any work may have a 'fear of failing.' These students may know enough to get by, 'coasting' in your sessions. But as the work gets harder, they slow down, procrastinating or completing only the easiest tasks. They sometimes mask their anxiety as bravado, getting very defensive when you push them towards their limits. These learners need to become more 'gritty' and learn that failure is part of the process. — refer to the chapter "Teach Grit" for more details.

3. Your Students May Have Challenges That Stop Them Learning

If you teach students who suffer from any physical, mental and emotional conditions and they are not feeling well, then this will have

THE BAD

a negative impact on the work that they produce. As a teacher, you will have to make allowances for these challenges. Depending on the nature of their difficulty, your student may be triggered by events and people, changing their state rapidly and they could present disruptive behaviours that can be difficult to manage. All of these things may happen before they set foot into your classroom. If this is an issue then you need to get some support. In the chapter "Assemble Your Team" I will cover that in detail.

4. You Don't Have A Relationship with The Student

This is very common when a new student is transferred to your class. If they are either a Disrupter or a Complaint, then they will be testing the waters with you. They will see what they can get away with and what they can't. Don't be surprised if at first, they may not follow what you say. Once you have done your homework on your students, you will learn what works and what doesn't.

These are not the only reasons and this list is not exhaustive. I'm sure that you can add your own to the mix. These examples are just illustrations to demonstrate that you must understand the root causes to be able to give the right responses. Hone your detective skills.

I know this has been flogged to death in other books but it well worth mentioning in our text — the best way to set milestones is by using SMART objectives. It's practical, quick and you don't have to be a nuclear physicist to set it up.

SMART stands for:

- **Specific** - get them to target a particular area or do a specific task
- **Measurable** - give them a way that you can measure the work has been done
- **Achievable** - make sure that they can actually hit this target at their current skill level
- **Relevant** - make sure that the work that they are being set will help them achieve the objective in the long run. Do not

give them unnecessary work to 'keep them busy.'
- **Time-bound** - give them a clear deadline to complete their task.

Getting your students to do something is always better than them doing nothing. People start as they mean to go on. Legendary psychologist Robert Cialdini in his groundbreaking book "Influence" described this characteristic as "The Law of Consistency."

Cialdini through extensive research discovered that most people, once they have made a decision, will follow through and stick to that decision for all similar choices. For example, if I commit daily to doing ten press-ups every day, I will be more likely to do fifteen press-ups the following week. Cialdini writes "once we have made a choice or taken a stand, we will encounter personal and interpersonal pressures to have to behave consistently with that commitment. Those pressures will cause us to respond in ways that justify our earlier decision."[5] If you can persuade someone to do a small thing like write three lines, in time, you can convince them to do bigger things like write a whole page.

Confusion equals disruption. As you train to be a teacher, you will be taught how to successfully differentiate your lessons for mixed ability learners, set high expectations and measure progress through different modes of assessment. This is beyond the scope of this chapter. But a book that I would thoroughly recommend is *Teaching Backwards* by Andy Griffith and Mark Burns. It has been an excellent resource that will help you square off these essential parts of your teaching practice.

Reflection Questions

1. Do you have students who regularly refuse to engage in any tasks? Do you know why? What approaches have you taken to get them going?
2. If you have students that state that the work is either too complicated or easy, have you planned to differentiate the tasks to their level? If you already have, how have they responded? If the option is available, do you feel that the

THE BAD

student may benefit from being in a different set or having a different teacher?
3. Do you have students that procrastinate often? What ways do they avoid doing the work that you set? Does this change when they sit next to other students?

Practical Tips

- If you have students who are either perfectionists or scared of failing in any of your classes, talk to them about how they should learn to "enjoy the process" rather than "getting to the result." Your students should understand that failing and coming up short is part of the learning process. See the chapter "Teach Grit" for more details.
- If you have a student that is very reluctant to try anything, try this old sales classic called the "Puppy Dog Close." If a pet store owner wanted a customer to buy a puppy and was met with resistance, the owner would simply tell the customer that they could take the puppy home, just for the night. If they were unhappy with the little cutie, they could return the puppy and receive a full refund, with no questions asked. Most of the time, if the pet store owner could get the customer to agree to try it for one night, chances are they would keep the dog. Ask your student to try a very, very little part of the task. If they complete that tiny step, they will be rewarded, regardless of the outcome. Make the step as small as it needs to be to get them to put pen to paper. Remember it's about getting them to engage at this stage, the quality will come later.
- If there is nothing wrong with the student and they are being rude, aggressive or uninterested, and you have tried all the techniques above, then a sanction may have to be given. Try the "The Easy Road or The Hard Road" technique. See the chapter "Be Just, Fair and Firm" for more details.

Use Your Windows Effectively

When we are teaching our students, we are fighting for their attention and chances are, 90% of the time, we have already lost the battle. Your students, especially if they are teenagers, are dealing with all that 'coming of age' stuff: trying to figure themselves out, thinking about their latest crush, wanting to fit in with the 'cool crew,' wondering whether to buy chicken and chips on the way home and so on.

But it doesn't end there. We are the first generation of teachers in our 200,000 year human history that are competing for our students' hearts and minds with a five by three inch flashing box that now dictates most of our lives. For the greatness of teachers like Socrates, Plato, Sir Isaac Newton or Richard Feynman, I don't know how they would cope with the constant ping, ping, ping of their students' mobile phones. From my experience, around 70% of the problems in my classroom have involved a mobile phone. Thank you, Steve Jobs.

The Independent Newspaper published an interesting article reporting that the average British adult in a meeting, can only concentrate for fourteen minutes at a time. According to their report, this got even worse if the meeting was more complex stating that "finance related meetings or conversations only keep our attention for 10 minutes[3]."

Our attention spans are getting shorter. If, as adults, we find it hard to concentrate for ten minutes, how much harder will it be to get our young people to focus for at least an hour?

When dealing with your students, you will find that there will be peaks and troughs in their attention and you must make sure that you use these 'windows' of attention effectively. Several factors affect the size of the windows.

- The time of day - In the mornings we are at our most refreshed and alert so we can concentrate for more extended periods. But as the day wears on, we get tired and these windows start to grow shorter. This is why, traditionally,

behaviour tends to worsen in the afternoons.
- The day of the week - If you teach students that have a full timetable, the cumulative effect of day to day lessons will wear your students down. By the time they reach Thursday or Friday, they will have their minds on the weekend rather than school.
- The classroom dynamics — if you have a class full of Compliants and Disrupters (see Chapter 'Positives, Compliants and Disrupters'), then the ability for your other students to concentrate on your tasks will be significantly reduced.

But before you learn how to take advantage of your windows, you will need to know how to think like a talent show host…

Read the Room

In a past life, when I used to present talent shows, one of the first skills I learnt on stage was to 'read the room'. I had to quickly be able to gauge the emotional state of the audience and adjust myself and my acts accordingly. For example, if the crowd was really antsy and wanted some hardcore hip-hop, putting RnB balladeer next on stage would probably cause a riot. My job allowed me to see what the elite performers did to win the crowd, up close and personal.

After hosting many shows, I started to notice a pattern that the budding stars initiated night after night. They talked to the crowd and asked them how they were that evening. They would have a fluid tracklist of around four songs and changed the order if they felt that one song would appeal to that particular audience, cutting the songs short if they thought that they were getting bored or irritated. Sometimes if they were really confident, they would ask the crowd what types of songs they wanted to hear, taking suggestions and then exceeding their fans expectations. These guys and gals were the ultimate professionals and they knew how to get the crowd on their side — they were stagecraft masters.

As teachers, we are the performers, and our classrooms are the stages. We control the emotional climate of classrooms for good or ill. Classes, like audiences, are ever changing: they can be hyper, subdued, aggressive, passive and everything in between. Adding new students or removing current ones could completely change the dynamic in an instant.

You must always keep your bunny ears up to see what is happening with your groups. Your students are like you… human. They go through ups and downs in their attention span, and can be either unsettled or really excited by outside events.

This is where your emotional intelligence and the relationships that you have with your students is critical — especially if you have students that can be quite challenging behaviour-wise. If you read the mood early and identify the students that are slightly 'off', this can help you prevent a 'flashpoint' situation.

This can be doubly important if you have students with SEMH needs. If you have students that are prone to severe mood swings that may disrupt the class, nine times out of ten, you will be able to spot this at the beginning of the lesson. With the knowledge that you have gathered from your relationships, you should have strategies in place like timeout cards, stress balls or additional one-to-one time with the Teaching Assistant to help keep the disruption to a minimum.

This all starts from the moment that they step through your door. The start of your lesson is absolutely critical to how the rest of your session will turn out. The best teachers I know, often have a routine that their students practice on how they enter and leave a room. If your students enter the room like the rhinos in *Jumanji*, then you will have an uphill struggle to get them under control. Stand by the door and get them settled *before* they come in. If you have any Compliants or Disrupters in your class, use the time outside to assess what emotional state they are in and whether this may have a negative impact on your classroom. Trust your instincts.

Here are some tips that will help you to take advantage of these windows and minimise any potential disruption.

THE BAD

'Front-load' Your Lessons

In music production, there is a technique called "front-loading" where the song will start off with the chorus or the hook such as Bob Marley's "I Shot The Sheriff" or Taylor Swift's "Bad Blood." This helps grab the listener's attention straight away.

Likewise, with your lessons, try to do your main activities as soon as possible, especially if they are the most labour-intensive. Your students' willpower will be at its strongest at the beginning of the lesson so take advantage of their fresh attention and energy.

Researchers have noted how willpower and attention span are directly related to the glucose that you had in your bloodstream. They reported that "willpower, like a muscle, becomes fatigued from overuse but can also be strengthened over the long term." [6] Start early and after the starter, hit them with the most tricky tasks first. If they do start to falter later in the lesson, you have completed the most important activities and you can rest a little easier.

Work Hard in Short Bursts

The best way to do this is by using the "Pomodoro Technique" and has been a mainstay in my teaching practice. This technique was developed by productivity expert and consultant Francesco Cirillo in the late 1980s. The word 'pomodoro' is Italian for 'tomato' and describes the tomato-shaped cooking timers that are still extremely popular today.

Set up the task, define the objectives and let your students to work for twenty-five minutes uninterrupted and with no distractions. Set the timer and display it somewhere that they can see it and keep them on task if they get distracted. After the timer stops, make sure that you give your learners a five-minute break. Although twenty-five minutes isn't a huge window, if done regularly, will help your students learn to focus and stay on task.

Other benefits include greater resilience to stress and time pressure. Dr Barbara Oakley writes in her book *A Mind For Numbers* that "if you learn under mild stress, you can handle greater stress more easily... if you get used to figuring things out under a mild time crunch, you are less likely to choke later, when you are in a high-pressure test-taking situation[7]." If you teach the same group of students over the year and they are preparing for an important test, you can gradually make the work intervals longer to simulate the exam conditions. That way, they are less likely to feel anxious in the real thing.

With the breaks, use lighter activities such as quizzes or group work. From my experience, allowing your students to stop completely makes it harder for your students to regain focus for the next big task. The aim here is to get their attention off the hard exercise to give them a chance to refresh their minds and willpower. Experiment and see what works for you.

Incentivise Your Lessons

If you have students who have worked diligently for the entire lesson, make sure that you reward them. As I said in the Chapter "Give Them Praise", make sure you reward them based more on their effort rather than their ability.

Make sure that the rewards are age appropriate and they will be enjoyed. Offering a "Gold Star" to a moody sixteen year old for good work will probably earn you their contempt rather than admiration, so be mindful of their preferences. Once you have got to know your students, you will figure out what will work for that cohort.

What I have found that works universally across the age ranges in 'free- time.' I let my students know that if they complete all their tasks to a good standard, they can get some time to do their own activities, either at the end of the lesson or at a future date.

Once you have agreed on a system with your students, monitor it and stick to it. Students who are really on board will learn how to organise themselves better to complete their tasks earlier — which helps them to be more independent and confident.

Reflection Questions

1. Do you find that your students are easily distracted? If so, what is the source of their distractions? How do your

learners enter your room? What steps have you taken to police their behaviour outside your space?
2. Throughout your lessons, do you find that your students tire and cannot focus? Does this change depend on the point in the day or the day of the week? Do you find that certain activities tire them out faster than others? Which ones?
3. Do you reward your students for their efforts? If so, how do you do it and has it worked well for you? If not, why not? Could you introduce a reward scheme? What things do your students like?

Practical Tips

- This tip is super simple. As your students enter the room or the hall, observe how they come in and compare it against what you usually see. If they are unusually hyper, then perhaps it would be best to do activities to calm them down, like getting them to line up quietly outside the classroom or to read in silence straight away. If they are unusually quiet or disengaged, have some icebreakers or quick activities ready. Don't ignore — if you don't get the start right, the rest of the lesson may suffer.
- There are thousands of timers on the Web. There is even a digital version of a "Pomodoro Timer" —I personally find the constant ticking really annoying, but have a gander. If you have a particularly tricky class, you can start with intervals as small as five minutes. The aim is to get them working solidly and then build up from there.
- Invest in a reward scheme for your students if you don't already have it, and if it's lame then do your own. Obviously, follow the procedures set by your institution but, where possible, give your students something to get excited about. Remember that "Fun" is on the Social Contract and make good on your promise — this goes a heck of a long way in making a positive vibe in your class. Please use common sense too — don't spend ludicrous amounts of money on

prizes or treats. Emptying your bank account is not fun for anyone but an age-appropriate movie, a tin of chocolates and free time are all inexpensive but work wonders. Be creative!

- If I am given a one-hour time block to teach a lesson, I imagine that I have forty-five minutes to explain the actual material and use the spare fifteen minutes to give my students breaks and perhaps some free-time. I had to do this with my NEET students because of the severity of the learning difficulties and to compensate for any unforeseen disruptions. But this framework has served me well in mainstream education too. Where possible, 'block' parts of your lessons so you have one or two main sections to teach and have breaks in between.

THE BAD

Check Your Body Language

When I was a kid, I loved Michael Jackson's stage performances. Michael could come on stage, not sing a word and flick his foot out and the crowd could go wild — he understood that his body, as well as his voice, sold his brand. Your body is continuously screaming what state that you are in and like everything else, you must learn to use it as a tool to help your students.

I am not a world expert on Body Language. Although I have researched and used a lot of these practices, I do realise that there are numerous factors involved in how your body language is received such as your gender, race, height, location, culture and so on. I would advise that you take these tips and experiment with them, look at the resources that I will provide at the end of the chapter and do your research.

Subconsciously, your body is unceasingly scanning the environment and reacting to any events that occur around you. When you feel happy, safe and content, your body will respond in a different way to when you feel anxious or aggravated, and sometimes this can happen without you even being aware that it has occurred.

Generally, the happier you are, the more relaxed and 'open' you would be in your body movements. Think of a time that you were at a summer barbecue surrounded by people that you love — how did you feel? You felt relaxed with no tension in your shoulders and jaw. When you spoke, you sat where ever you wanted, walking around the garden without a care in the world. You used your hands a lot more and were not shy to let out a loud laugh or raise your voice especially when you are telling a joke.

Now compare this when you are going for a tough job interview in a place that you didn't know. You kept your hands to your side or fiddled with your phone to mask your anxiety. When you sat down, you took up as little space as possible, and you sat somewhere out of the way. When you met new people, you measured your words and talked in a softer tone. You were more conscious of the space around you and concerned with how people perceived you. In this state, you felt more guarded or 'closed.'

Finally, I want you to think about a person of importance that has a powerful physical presence. Take a minute to do this. Got it? Now I want you to think about that person's body language.

For me, it's former US President Barack Obama: from his confident, commanding walk to his glowing grin, he carried himself with authority but simultaneously had grace and a coolness that endeared him to people all around the world. For most of his presidency, Obama was charismatic, focused and never seemed to lose control. In the next section let's look at some of the things that will hopefully give you a piece of his magic.

Body Talk

Human beings have evolved to become excellent readers of body language. Your students are always comparing what you say versus what you do.

To be authoritative and be able to have the respect of your class, your words and your body must be singing off the same hymn-sheet. We will cover the particulars of using our voices in the next chapter, but we will generally look at the other parts that make up your non-verbal communication here.

Physical Space

The physical distance between people, to observers, tells us a lot about the dynamics of a relationship. Think of two people who are genuinely in love and how they may walk together compared to two people who are ready to break up. In a typical office, you would usually be able to tell who had authority by the way they move around the space compared to those who are lower on the pecking order.

The space in our immediate vicinity is particularly important to us. But why is this? Neuroscientist Michael Graziano in an interview for *National Geographic Magazine* explained why we are so obsessed by our 'peripersonal space.' Graziano stated, "the brain computes a buffer zone around the body, which is very flexible. It changes in size, depending on context, computed in a manner that's largely unconscious... The invisible second skin is primarily protection. It has a huge range of functions. It can be as basic as protecting you

THE BAD

against an actual physical threat, like a predator."[8]

Although we have mobile phones, internet and lots of fancy gadgets, our nervous system has not changed from when our ancestors were hunter-gathers hundreds of thousands of years ago. Whereas most of us no longer have to worry about lions and wolves in the modern age, when someone threatening approaches us, our body reacts like we are about to be eaten alive and this not helpful.

Why is this relevant to you as a teacher? That's simple: how you interact with the space in your classroom displays your state of being. It's about dominance — if you are an 'authority' in your subject, then you should act the part. To paraphrase Denzel Washington in *Training Day*, King Kong should have nothing on you.

If you are the type of teacher that tends to either stay behind your desk, stick to the corners of the room and act like you shouldn't be there, this could display signs that you are nervous and frightened. Why do people put pictures of their loved ones on their desks? It makes them feel more comfortable being somewhere different from their homes.

Walk around with confidence, head held high, shoulders straight and be bold in YOUR class. Sit in different places, walk and talk in the centre of the room, and use your hands to articulate your main points for impact. Sometimes you will teach an individual or a class that makes you feel intimidated — despite how you feel, do these things anyway. It's a two-way relationship with your body — if you do the things physically that display confidence, you will feel it in your mind too. You have my permission to fake it until you make it.

Be mindful of how people enter your personal space and vice versa. Working with NEET students taught me the importance of getting the balance right. In the early days, they used the peripersonal space as a way to display dominance. The more challenging students would try to stand within breathing distance of me and refuse to move. This was the cause of many firefights. Students must not enter your personal space without permission. This is an act of aggression and must not be tolerated at all.

Enforce your boundaries and make it clear that they are crossing a line. The same thing applies if you have students doing it to each other. These acts tend to make people feel unsafe, and your students need to be educated on why this is prohibited.

We must also be mindful of our body positioning when we interact with our students. Where possible, always talk to them on their physical level when you are not teaching the whole class. For example, if a student asks you an individual question about their work and they are sitting down, try to either kneel down or grab a seat next to them — obviously not too close. Standing over people for the reasons I already outlined above, can be intimidating and may cause the student to react aggressively. Mirroring their physical position shows that you are there to help, not to harm.

Hands

If you want to tell how someone is feeling, look at their hands. Have you ever had a time when you hand to make an important presentation and you were really nervous? What were your hands doing? If you were like me, your hands were probably shaking — as the kids would say 'that's not a good look.' Here are some tips to help you to 'handle' your business.

- Avoid fidgeting and keep things out of your hands — when we are nervous we to like to drum on things, fiddle with pens, rustle our notes or rub our hands together. Etiquette expert Rosalinda Oropeza Randall, in an interview for the Business Insider UK, stated that "while these behaviours have a soothing effect, they can take the focus away from what you are saying and may look a little 'too close for comfort' for the watchers."[9] Your nervous hands make you the equivalent of a frightened deer in the headlights. Practice having your hands to the side, which is known as the neutral stance. If you still cannot control your hands, try putting them behind your back like a military general or a policeman. This type of position can show power and authority and help hide your nervousness.
- Learn how to 'box' - Try to keep your hands roughly in the 'box' — this roughly is the area between the top of your chest to the bottom of your abdomen which is where your button belly button is. If you are consistently flailing your arms like

- Kermit the Frog, it can be a little distracting. Keep your hands centred most of the time.
- Learn how to gesture - As an audience, our brains love nothing more than when the speaker's words and hand actions match up. This reinforces the message that is being conveyed and gives your speech that extra 'oomph.' Human psychology website "scienceofpeople.com" reported that the most popular videos that are viewed on TED.com were given by speakers who used lots of hand gestures. The investigation concluded that "the bottom TED Talks had an average of 124,000 views and used an average of 272 hand gestures during the 18 minute talk. The top TED Talks had an average of 7,360,000 views and used an average of 465 hand gestures—that's almost double[10]." Things like counting down with your hands, measuring, using push and pull gestures can make you more captivating and more likely that your listeners take in the message.
- Use your palms — your palms can be great communication tools. Having your palms up facing upwards when you speak can signal, cooperation, surrender, humility and need. Open palms indicate trust. On the other hand, having your palms down facing downwards, suggests that something is decided or final. Many famous orators would either 'pat down' or slam their hands on their desks to show their displeasure or emphasise their points forcefully. Watch your palms.

Eyes

Make sure that you maintain eye contact with your students. When you are in front of your class, make sure that you are looking at different students at different points in the room. Do not be afraid to walk around the room at the same time. Your ability to maintain eye contact shows your confidence and authority. Please note: do not stare too long as it could make you look a bit creepy or could be seen as an act of aggression. Use this power wisely.

Reflection Questions

1. In your classroom, do students tend to violate physical boundaries? How does this play out in your class? Do you tend to ignore it or call it out?
2. When you feel nervous or anxious, body-wise what do you tend to do? Do you feel more "open" or "closed?" What strategies do you use to make yourself feel more comfortable when you are afraid or irritated?
3. Do you tend to move around the classroom or stay fixed to one spot? Why is that? Do you engage in eye contact with your students?

Practical Tips

- From my experience, I would say that 70% of altercations that happen in the classroom would revolve around the violation of other people's boundaries. Some students may touch other students inappropriately as a joke, but this often leads to bigger problems. Personal space must be taken very seriously and that includes yours. When drawing up your Social Contract make sure that this is a major point of the discussion.
- What I have written here is merely touching the surface of non-verbal communication. There are thousands of resources on the Internet that can help you understand it further. There are two sources that I would thoroughly recommend for your continued study: At the time of writing, there is a fantastic YouTube channel called "Charisma On Command" that is run by body language expert Charlie Houpert. He posts scores of videos that look at the ways that you can appear more confident, magnetic and authoritative. It has been incredibly useful to me and very actionable. Another great resource that I would recommend is a book called *What Every Body Is Saying* by Ex FBI Agent Joe Navarro. It is a brilliant book that allows you to decipher

THE BAD

human body language and full of plenty of exercises that you can do straight away.
- I know that this is incredibly uncomfortable to most of us, but try to see if you can get a colleague or a manager to film you while you are teaching. It's horrible at first but you will always find something beneficial. Most of our actions are subconscious so we are not even aware that we are doing them! Give it a try even for five minutes and I am sure that you will find something that will help you improve. Or if you simply can't take being on camera, get a colleague or manager to observe you in your class, focusing on your presence and movement.

Talk With Authority

What do Bill Clinton, Winston Churchill, Adolf Hitler, Fidel Castro, Joseph Goebbels, Martin Luther King Jr, Ronald Reagan, Margaret Thatcher, Benazir Bhutto and Queen Elizabeth I have in common? These individuals all had reputations for being fantastic public speakers. For good or ill, these orators could influence entire nations to follow their causes and effect massive change. Although you may not be a national leader (well not yet), you are still in a position of influence, and I have good news for you: many of these skills can be learnt.

Speaking = Leadership

If you want to be a good leader, you need to be a good communicator. When we think of great orators, we think of speakers with soaring, flowery speeches that take us to heaven and back, but great communicators come in all shapes, sizes and tones.

Where does this come from? Why do human beings place so much emphasis on those who can speak and lead well? Researchers Allen Garbo, Brian Spisak and Mark van Vugt attempted to answer this question in a fascinating study called "Charisma as Signal: An Evolutionary Perspective on Charismatic Leadership." The authors argued that we tended to follow these great communicators because they clearly spelt out the norms and values that the group should follow and helped to make these values continue to stick.

From an evolutionary perspective, speakers would be necessary when trying to coordinate a team to complete a difficult task like taking down a fierce woodland bison: a job that a single person could not do on their own.

The authors use the example of a stag hunt to illustrate this dilemma. If you have a group who are hunting a stag, you must be absolutely sure that you are all committing 100% to kill the animal. Any hesitation or mistakes could be fatal. Plus, you must make sure that your actions are coordinated, to ensure that you do this quickly and efficiently. That takes someone that could lead, communicate and spell out a cohesive plan. If you are in a group led by this type of leader, the authors state "the decision to cooperate becomes a more rational strategy because it is reasonable to assume that, no matter whom one's partner is, they are likely to have heard the same speeches, felt the same emotions, shared a similar vision, and been reminded of the same values or norms of behaviour." [11] In other words, you will know that John or Nicole won't skewer you from behind with their spear when you are hunting your dinner. Leaders that can talk effectively become great focal points that the group can follow.

Now you know the background, let's look at some ways that we can improve the way we talk.

KISS - Keep It Simple Stupid

Get to the point. Don't waffle and make your instructions crystal clear. When we are nervous, we tend to ramble or 'talk in circles': think of a time where you wanted to ask your boss for a promotion or that cute work colleague for a date. Often our message becomes lost and confused, and we don't come across very well, which damages our authority. The best leaders can take a complex subject and make it simple and accessible enough to be understood by all.

At this time of writing, Donald J. Trump is the 45th President of the United States of America. His no-nonsense, New York style has made him loved as much as hated in his home country and beyond. His unpredictable actions, statements and tweets have made him an international figure of controversy the world over. Still - I'm not here to talk politics, but to learn from the man known as 'The Donald.'

Despite what our personal feelings are about him, his 2016 election campaign showed us a skill that Donald Trump is an absolute master at: the ability to craft simple yet powerful messages that managed to shock, entertain but ultimately dominate the media coverage, always keeping him front and centre in the public's consciousness.

In 2016, one of his main campaign messages was to take stricter measures against illegal immigrants. He focused his sights squarely on the illegal Mexicans who were entering America through the Texas border, located in the south of the country. So, what was Donald's solution to such the political minefield that has dogged US politics for decades? It was very simple: The US would build the wall to keep the illegal immigrants out and get the Mexicans to pay for it. That's it, really.

"Build The Wall" became one of his key campaign slogans and would fire up his supporters into a frenzy whenever he said those three words. But his opponents were very rightly sceptical. To make this promise work, America would build a 1,900 mile-wide, 50ft tall barrier. According to the BBC, a report which was conducted by the Washington Post stated that the wall could cost $25bn. [12]

Absolutely ridiculous, right? His opponents ridiculed him for such a silly statement. But some eagle-eyed observers saw what Trump was doing and how effective it was. Scott Adams, the genius behind the successful Dilbert comics, believed that most critics were missing the point. Adams wrote "If Trump had wanted to be accurate, he would have mentioned all the solutions every time he talked about security... When they were done critiquing Trump for the 'error' for saying he would build one big solid 'wall,' the critics had convinced themselves that border security was a higher priority than they had thought coming into the conversation... It also sucked up media energy that might have been focused on political topics he didn't understand at the same depth as his competitors[13]." In other words, Trump's simple "Build The Wall" soundbite set the agenda and pushed everything out of the way.

His ability to come up with clear, snappy slogans, no matter how crazy, allowed him to absorb all the media attention, control the conversation, force his opponents to be on the back foot and this ultimately gave him the keys to the White House.

How does this help you? Make your messages clear, concise and to the point especially when dealing with bad behaviour. Don't get dragged into fruitless arguments or issues you don't understand. Stay professional and polite but don't be ambiguous and indecisive. If your students have crossed a line, let them know without any hesitation. Being polite yet frank will help you build a good reputation that will enhance your authority. Be a straight shooter.

THE BAD

Avoid Filler

Although we may teach every day, when we are anxious, we can display some behaviours that can work against us and can take away our authority. Imagine 'em' that I 'ah' was saying this 'um' sentence 'em' out 'ah' loud — it would 'um' be 'ah' really, really 'em' annoying. These constant 'umming' and 'ahhing' are known as "speech disfluencies" and these can wreak havoc on your presentations and teaching time. Other types of speech disfluencies include:

- Overuse of certain words and phrases like 'you know', 'well', 'you understand?', 'so'
- Do-overs - this is where you may stumble or mispronounce a particular word and keep on repeating it until you get it right
- Mind blocks — where the sentence that you had in your mind disappears and you are stumped on what to say next.

We have all seen it. The person who is on stage and is totally overcome by stage fright. It's excruciating to watch and worse to experience. Here's a couple of tips that can help you.

- Slow down — when we are faced with a situation that makes us afraid or irritated, we tend to speed up and our voice tends to go up a couple of pitches. If this happens when you are speaking, take a breath and slow down. Speak slowly and deliberately. If you analyse the most prolific public speakers, when they are faced with a tough question, they pause, clarify what the person is asking and speak confidently and transparently. You can't do that if you're speaking faster than Sonic the Hedgehog.
- Chunk the information that you teach — think of a presentation that you have seen that has made you want to go to sleep. The speaker was probably a master of DBP - Death By PowerPoint. Avoid just relying on reading off a slide or a book as this can be boring for everyone. Organise your session in 'chunks' and work on how you will transition from one chunk to another. Where most people may lose

their train of thought and get an attack of the 'filler-blues' is during the times that they are moving from one section to another. In each chunk make sure that you know your objectives and leave some space for some magic to happen. See the chapter "Don't Be Boring" for more details.

- Know your stuff - I know that you are an expert in your field and you keep up to date with all goings-on in your subject. But when the syllabus changes or we have to do something that is outside of our preplanned lessons, we can feel out of our depth. Sometimes it may not even be your lessons or subject matter that may be changing, but the way that you deliver your sessions via a new piece of technology. Whatever the case may be, if you feel that you are uncertain in your lessons, this will come through in the way that you talk. Make sure that you have a couple of dry runs before you take it into a live class.

Use Silence As Your Friend

For reasons that I will explain later, I am not a great fan of ranting at your students. Excessive shouting, moaning and complaining not only puts you in a negative headspace, but I have found that this strategy over time stops working. Infamous author and modern-day Machiavelli, Robert Greene stated, "by stating less than necessary, you create the appearance and meaning of power. Also the less that you say, the less risk you run of saying something foolish, even dangerous[14]."

This is something else that I learnt from my sales days — silence can be just as powerful as using your voice. Professional public speakers are taught that before they speak on stage, after the crowd has settled down, they should take a couple of seconds before they start their speech. This serves two purposes: it allows them to soothe their nerves and embrace the stage and helps the crowd to focus their attention on the speaker by creating a little tension.

If you have a particularly loud class, shouting at them increases the noise level and you are reacting rather than being proactive. If they seem like they are not ready to listen, stay silent and just put the minutes on the board until they settle down. Tell them that the minutes that you have wasted will be paid back in the form of a lunchtime detention or an after-school revision session. Your students must learn how to value your time.

Reflection Questions

1. Do you ever feel tongue-tied? Does this constantly happen or at particular times? Does this happen during times of stress?
2. When you have to correct behaviour, does your voice change or stay the same? Do you feel that you are authoritative, or do you think that you are being reactive?
3. How do you feel being silent? Are you the type of person who needs to fill uncomfortable silences with additional words or can you sit back and observe? Do you have to repeatedly shout to get your classes attention? How does that feel?

Practical Tips

- Pauses are really powerful when you are faced with tricky situations. Rather than going into "firefighting" mode, a small pause can allow you to collect your thoughts and think of your next response and make you seem more confident too. There is a difference between saying "John stop talking!" And "John. Stop talking." The second response sounds more composed and more assured. Try it and see.
- Think of a lesson that didn't go well. Look at the lesson plan. How elaborate was your plan? How well did you explain these concepts? Great teachers make the complex simple. If your students continue to struggle with your material, you may need to strip the idea down to its simplest level and then build it up from there.
- I would be an absolute hypocrite if said that I never raised my voice. Sometimes the class is boisterous and you need to get the class' attention quickly. Other times, there may be

dangers or hazards that the students may not be aware of and you need to be heard quickly. If you do raise your voice, always be mindful why you are doing it. If you are shouting to rant, vent or to try get some form of retribution then you have been 'emotionally hijacked.' Make sure you are using it for the right reasons — stay in control.

The Ugly

Beware Of The Emotional Hijack

We have all had our moments. You know the ones. As you are driving on the road with your family, a crazy driver comes out of nowhere and narrowly misses your car. Or you are waiting in the queue in the supermarket and some moron barges in front of you, without a single word and a smirk on his face. Your heart starts beating loudly, your fists clench, your eyes narrow, you feel tightness in your chest, your mouth opens and something horrible comes out. The driver and the queue jumper do the same thing and before you know it, you have entered Stupidland, the Home of the Dumb.

You end up having a nasty argument (or worse). Days later, after some reflection, you look back in horror wondering why you acted in such a reckless manner.

My friend, you have been emotionally hijacked.

Don't beat yourself up folks. That is the way that we were wired. Although we can upgrade our smartphones every eighteen months, as a species, our brains are ancient and there are no software upgrades available. Our bodies would treat an angry student the same way that we would treat a velociraptor in *Jurassic Park* which is no good for anybody. Before we go into talking about how to handle a situation let's have a brief conversation on how our nervous system works.

Your Nervous System

I am not going to go into extreme scientific detail, and I am sure that some Biology students will spit out their tea in frustration after they read this section. But I want to give a straightforward overview of how our nervous system works and how this applies to your classroom.

Your brain is the most complex organism in the known universe.

This organ is an astonishing piece of biological machinery — there are different parts of your brain that interlink and interconnect. Our brain has one primary function — which is to keep you alive at all costs.

If your brain sees something and interprets it as dangerous, this spooks a part of your grey matter known as 'amygdala', which is in charge of our emotions, including fear. This sends a signal to the 'hippocampus', which is in charge of most of our involuntary functions such as our breathing, heart rate and blood pressure.

If the hippocampus is alerted, it activates something known as the Sympathetic Nervous System (SNS), which pumps a cocktail of powerful hormones into your bloodstream, including adrenaline, which gives you a burst of energy that will help you deal with the threat. Think of the SNS as the accelerator in a car. These hormones force your heart to beat faster forcing more blood into your muscles. The airways in your lungs open wider to allow you to take in more air and this causes you to breathe more heavily.

Your body also releases glucose into your bloodstream, giving you fuel for the fight. All these changes can happen in milliseconds — so fast that sometimes we can react to something faster than we can mentally process it.

Once the threat has gone or you have escaped, the Parasympathetic Nervous System (PNS) kicks in. The PNS is the opposite of the SNS and acts of the body's "brake" and sends messages to your body that will help it to relax. The PNS will lower your heart rate, slows down your breathing and will send blood to your intestines which will help you digest your food. The PNS is a lot slower to kick in that the SNS and your body will need time to return back to its restful state.

Both systems act as counterbalances to each other: if your SNS was too overactive, you would have a heart attack, and if PNS was allowed to run free, your heart rate would lower to the point that it would stop beating. Nature is a beautiful thing.

Fight, Flight or Freeze

Unless you are a world class yoga teacher, you will not have a problem with your Parasympathetic Nervous System - it's the SNS that causes the biggest issues in the classroom. When we are in that heightened state, we tend to fall into one of these three responses.

Fight

If you are presented with a perceived threat from a student or situation, your body gets you ready to fight back. Your body's nervous system is twitching harder than a child watching to a grime music video. You are 'firefighting.' This is where it starts to kick off. Symptoms of the 'Fight' response could include:

- Personal space invasion
- Shouting
- Slamming doors or throwing things in frustration
- Stomping around the room
- Clenching of fists or teeth
- Becoming more argumentative and talking over people

Obviously, as a teacher, this would be the worst response that you could display and potentially the most dangerous.

Flight

In this state, you just want to come out of the situation as fast as possible. Everything in your body is screaming at you to "get out of there!" If something looks too big to fight or is simply just too overwhelming, your body wants you to get the hell out of Dodge. Symptoms of this state include:

- Being fidgety — shaking limbs and constant tapping on the floor or the table
- Not staying still — constant squirming while sitting down or walking around the room
- Backing off — the individual will put distance between them and the threat by using objects like tables or chairs
- Rapid breathing
- Wide eyes, constantly looking around, feeling on high-alert

Freeze

If you can't 'fight' and 'flight' is not an opinion, you will just 'freeze.' In this state, you 'shut down' emotionally and mentally. In extreme cases, you may even go into shock. Symptoms include:

- Feeling 'spaced out' — the individual feels like they are 'not there' and they are not present
- Feeling numb or frozen
- Feeling like you have either lost your voice or the right words are not coming out of your mouth
- Not moving, or having a low response, no matter how extreme the situation is

Let me repeat; all these responses would be normal if you were in the middle of a war zone, facing a hungry lion or trying to survive after a devastating earthquake - but not in a classroom situation facing an angry pubescent teenager. Here are the downsides of being emotionally hijacked:

Your Intelligence and Problem-Solving Skills Can Drop Dramatically

Have you ever been a classroom situation where you reacted in a way that you shouldn't have? In your moments of reflection, have you ever racked your brains trying to understand what the hell you were thinking? In those moments, the issue is, you weren't thinking at all.

The National Institute for the Clinical Application of Behavioural Medicine (NICABM) reports "elevated cortisol causes a loss of neurons in the prefrontal cortex (PCF). Suppressed activity in the PFC prevents you from using your best judgement[1]." In other words, the thinking part of your brain turns off which means that you can't make good decisions. In a tense situation, you want to keep as clear-headed as possible.

When an ugly situation occurs, even the best of us may find that our emotional intelligence flies out of the window. Your thinking becomes narrow, and you may be so focused on the misbehaving student that you don't see the possible solutions.

You Lose Compassion and Stop Listening

As I mentioned at the beginning of this book, this book is mainly aimed at teachers and lecturers that deal with students aged between eleven and eighteen. These guys are a sub-species of human-beings called "teenagers." I know that they can be challenging to teach but being a teenager isn't easy. Especially if you understand what is happening in their minds.

In a study co-researched by Harvard University and the University of Washington, researchers found that teenagers have 'poor emotional differentiation.' Emotional differentiation is the ability to identify, label and cope with conflicting emotions. Teenagers are often bombarded with emotions that overlap and can overwhelm their developing nervous systems and this can lead to mood swings, tantrums and increased irritability.

Lead author Erik Nook stated "It's possible that increases in co-experienced emotions make it more difficult for teens to differentiate and regulate their emotions, potentially contributing to risk of mental illness[2]."

If you teach teenage students, you must remember that they are more prone to emotional hijacking because of the physiological changes in their body. As teachers, we must remain conscious that despite the difficulties our students may face, we must model the correct emotional responses and teach our students to do the same. If we are emotionally hijacked, we lose the capacity to hear, to understand and to teach our students how to express themselves healthily.

If Chronic, Can Lead to Bad Mental and Emotional Health

It's essential to understand being emotionally hijacked is meant to be only a temporary state. Unless you were a complete nutter, you wouldn't put yourself in the path of danger every single day.

But teaching can be taxing for even the best of us. If your SNS

THE UGLY

is activated continuously every time you enter a classroom, we can enter what Dr William G. Timms describes as a 'Chronic Stress Response.'

Dr Timms writes, "too much of any stress results in maladaptation at the biochemical level. Hormones become imbalanced and depleted... The systems of the body become compromised. Loss of vitality, illness and disease are the results[3]."[3] Emotional hijacks damage you over the long-term. Sadly, I have seen brilliant teachers leave the profession due to developing stress-related health issues. Constant stress will ruin your career and your life in the long run – don't let it.

In the chapter "How to Handle A Flashpoint," I will talk more about practical solutions for handling a crisis situation, but I really want to point out that it all starts from you. If you are not at your best, mentally, emotionally and physically, you cannot expect your class to be either. You are the driving force of your class. Part of having high emotional intelligence is knowing yourself and knowing when you are not OK.

In our job, we must keep on checking in with ourselves, and if we are struggling, we must have the courage to face this reality and find the resources and the help to get back on track. In our profession, sometimes we can be guilty of looking after everyone else's needs but our own — we must use the compassion and awareness that we show to our students equally ourselves. Any good athlete knows that rest and relaxation are just as important as practice and competition, and we must have the same mentality to stay at our peak.

Reflection Questions

1. How often in the classroom do you feel that you get emotionally hijacked? Is it with a particular class or with certain students? If so, who and why?
2. What is your fear response - fight, flight or freeze? How does this manifest physically? Are there any particular triggers and, if so, have you acted to mitigate them?
3. What things do you do to maintain your emotional, physical and mental health? When stressed, what things make you feel

better? Do you believe that your health has been affected by your work? What are you currently doing to reverse the trend?

Practical Tips

- When I was struggling with managing my life and work stress, I took up mindfulness and Tai Chi. Honestly, both those practices have been incredibly life-affirming and I have felt their benefits in every area of my life. I would encourage you to take up any method that allows you to calm your mind and be present. There are thousands of studies that show that many of these mind-body practices have real benefits to your overall wellbeing and can help get your SNS and PNS working more efficiently and less prone to emotional hijacks. Practices like prayer, Tai Chi and Yoga help centre you, and calm the traffic in the mind so that you can feel more confident, more relaxed and more alert. Try something and see what fits you and your lifestyle, you won't regret it. In the next chapter, I will break down specific techniques that will help you increase your wellbeing in your institution and beyond.
- Try not to take things personally. Teenagers are hard enough to deal with but when you have thirty of them, it can be a nightmare. Even your best students can have off days and you will be on the receiving end of these outbursts. Of course, sanction accordingly, but try not to take it on. Unless you are unlucky to have a particularly nasty student, most of them change their attitudes and moods like the weather, and it's inevitable that we get caught up in their storms. Once you walk off the premises, try to leave that day's troubles behind you. I know that it is easier said than done, but if you carry too much on your shoulders, your teaching career will seem more like a prison sentence than a job. Learn to let go of certain things.

- Awareness is key — if you find yourself in a flashpoint (which I promise you as a teacher you will), try to bring awareness to the situation. When you have Johnny Tableflipper in your face, it can all go south very quickly - but if anything, watch your breathing. That is one of the first things to go. Try to count just three breaths before you respond — it's not a lot but it's enough to keep you centred and help you weather the hurricane. Try it and see.

How Well Are You Maintaining Your Engine?

The Notorious M.O.T

I come from a family of real petrol heads — my siblings, cousins, aunties and uncles are the types that will sit there and calculate the cost per gallon, the braking torque and what is the metric horsepower of the engine shaft within every car they see on TV. I am not one of those people. Give me the car, show me how to drive, brake and park and I'm as happy as Kanye West on an awards stage. I will drive the car until the wheels fall off — literally.

One of the things I hate the most in the world is taking my car for its MOT. Once a year, UK car owners drag their vehicles to the mechanics to test if they are still road worthy according to the Ministry of Transport's standards. If your car passes with flying colours, then great! You just pay for the test, but if it fails then either you have to pay an arm and a leg for repairs, or you have to put the car down. The only thing I hate more than going to the mechanics is going to the dentist — but at least the dentist gives you free toothpaste. Maybe the mechanics can learn a thing or two…

But luckily, a couple of years back, a good friend of mine introduced me to my current mechanic, a gifted man called Mukesh. He has looked over every one of my cars for close to ten years, and my pockets have been better for it. Mukesh, over the years, taught me the early warning signs to look for when the car was ready to give up the ghost, and simple little tips and tricks that would help me keep the car on the road for longer.

Mukesh always preached the importance of looking after the engine of the car. Mukesh would always joke "people love to make the outside of the car look pretty but allow their engine to rot — these people will have pretty disasters." From then on, I have been 'pretty' consistent on making sure that my car's engine is well cared for (pun intended).

THE UGLY

Don't Be A 'Pretty' Disaster

In my life, I have realised that it's not only cars that are 'pretty disasters.' Unfortunately, many of us look good on the outside, but we are one incident away from completely breaking down on the side of Life's road. I have met many teachers who, because of the demands of the job, were treading water and hoping that they can make it through the day. I have seen teachers breakdown in tears in the staffroom because they just couldn't cope with the tsunami of tasks, meetings and books to mark. Then to top it off, Johnny Tableflipper and Mary Paperthrower kicked off in their class today.

This is the reality of the job. It's rewarding but can be a punishing vocation. Also, I am not saying this because I have always had everything under control - I too have experienced emotional and physical burnout through my career, and I needed to take time out to recover.

From my experience, most teachers go to work to make a genuine difference to the lives of their students — it's a calling, not a career. Teaching is one of those jobs that you can't just wing. You have to commit your mind, body, emotions to this gig.

But there is a dark side to this calling. Most of us don't show that same compassion to OURSELVES that we show our students, and that's a massive problem. Like the drivers Mukesh was talking about who only take care of the outside, we want to show the world that we are fine or doing 'better than ever,' but all our internal meters are in the red and every day we wonder how we are keeping it together.

We are perfectionists, constantly trying to improve our lessons and our craft. But when we make a small mistake, we brutally criticise ourselves and repeatedly use that mistake as a baseball bat to beat our mind to a pulp. We fight with the racing thoughts, anxiety and self-doubt daily. We yearn for our weekends and holidays, only to spend most of it in bed, dreading that Monday morning alarm when we have to do it all again. If this continues, then you face a real danger of damaging all aspects of your health, which that could become permanent and debilitating.

I told you I knew. If you have ever felt like this, then I am here to give you a virtual hug and tell you that it's OK not to feel OK.

These are all signs that you need to work on taking better care of yourself.

I know you too well. Some of you are thinking, "OK, Dalai Lama, what does all this fluffy stuff have to do with my teaching?" Well, here's the 411: if you run yourself into the ground, there is no way that you will be able to take care of your class, period. If you are exhausted or anxious when you enter that difficult classroom, you will NOT be able to teach and lead to the best of your abilities.

There is a reason why I put this chapter in the "Ugly" section. If you do not look after yourself, YOUR LIFE will be disrupted. I really cannot say it enough. In the last chapter, I spoke about 'emotional hijacking' and how this makes you appear in the classroom. In this chapter, we will look at the things that you can do to make sure that you are in Rocky II condition to face your class.

Like Mukesh, I want to go through a couple of ways to look after your mental, emotional and physical engine so that you can stay on the road longer and healthier in your teaching career and in your life.

Exercise

I really won't beat you over the head with this one. Everyone and their mother knows that exercise is the key to good health and performance. For the nerds out there (which includes me), here are some statistics that show the benefits of exercise:

- Exercise training can reduce trait anxiety and single exercise sessions can result in reductions in state anxiety
- Single sessions of moderate exercise can reduce short-term physiological reactivity to, and enhance recovery from, brief psychosocial stressors
- The anti-depressant effect of exercise can be of the same magnitude as found for other psychotherapeutic interventions.[4]

To simplify: exercise is good for your mind and helps you handle stress and other negative mental states such as anxiety and depression. But let me make one thing clear: I am not a fitness fanatic, and I don't go to the gym four times a week. My six-pack

THE UGLY

disappeared around 2008 and won't come back despite my desperate searches. But I do try to do at least twenty minutes of walking every day and work up a sweat everyone once in a while. Walking, especially after work, allows me to unwind and get some perspective. You don't have to run a marathon to get some exercise. Many things can help you work up a sweat, have some fun and help keep you healthy.

Sleep

There have been hundreds of scientific papers that state that without adequate sleep your brain cells can't work together correctly. In fact, Livescience.com reports that "inadequate sleep exerts a similar influence on our brain as drinking too much."[5] You wouldn't stagger into your class, slurring your speech and passing out on your desk and expect to have a good lesson — as well as keeping your job would you? Well, every time you don't sleep, you are doing the same thing. Get your daily seven to eight hours of sleep, try not to look at your phone in the middle of the night as this could disrupt your sleep pattern. Try to wake up and sleep at the same times every day and try to "power down" an hour before rest by doing something relaxing like meditating or listening to gentle music. The better the sleep you get, the better you can perform.

Nutrition

Your eating patterns can also affect your performance. Apart from making Fast-Food-R-Us happy, having big juicy cheeseburger every day will not only affect your gut but affect your brain too. Our body relies on a sugary substance called glucose that gives us energy during the day. Our stomach breaks down our food and the nutrients get released in the bloodstream. But when you eat foods full of fat or carbohydrates, this can cause problems for your thinking abilities. As the Harvard Business Review reports heavy meals like burgers and French fries will "provide more sustained energy, but require our digestive system to work harder, reducing oxygen levels in the brain and making us groggy."[6]

I am not a nutritionist or Joe Wicks - I am not going to tell you what you can or can't eat. But if you do notice that after breakfast or lunch you are feeling a bit tired or slightly out of sorts, it may be worth looking at having something lighter like a salad instead. When I was working with the NEETs, I needed every advantage I could get to keep my mental and physical edge. Try it and see what happens.

Positive Social Contact

Especially in the early days of your career, you may feel that you have to sacrifice certain things to get 'ahead.' You may put in the long hours at school, come home late at night to finish marking, scoff down your ready meal, catch a quick episode of your favourite Netflix show and then bed down for the night. Rinse and repeat. In the meantime, you may sacrifice time with your friends, colleagues and family. But over time, the lack of positive, non-work related contact can do severe damage to your health.

Positive Social Contact is any positive interactions with people who make you feel energised, safe, allows you to be yourself, warts and all. What are we working for anyway? My mum used to say "show me your friends and I and will tell you who you are", but I would now say "show me your friends and I and will tell you *how* you are."

Study after study has shown that positive social interaction with people who you like, love and respect helps battle anxiety, depression and helps you to recover faster from physical ailments. Positive relationships can help increase happiness, career prospects and even can extend your lifespan.

The Guardian newspaper looked at the research link between friendship and pain tolerance. They found that when people are in healthy, stable relationships, their bodies produced endorphins that killed pain and made them feel good too. One of the lead researchers, Katherine Johnson, stated: "at an equivalent dose, endorphins have been shown to be stronger than morphine." [7] Morphine - the painkiller they give to you after you have major surgery — that is saying something. Other hormones like oxytocin, dopamine and serotonin can help flush out all the harmful chemicals that are in our system after an emotional hijack and make us bounce back faster as a result.

I know that we want to work hard but make sure that you get the chance to spend time with your friends and family. Being a better friend, husband, wife, partner, parent, son, daughter, niece, nephew (you get the idea) can ultimately make you a better teacher. Never underestimate the power of friendship — the Care Bears didn't and neither should you.

Reflection Questions

1. How well have you been 'maintaining your engine' while you have been working? Are you a 'pretty disaster' and finding it difficult to manage the daily stresses of teaching? What have you done so far to stop you hitting your limit and has it been effective?
2. How much sleep do you get every night? If you get less than seven hours of sleep, why is that? Do you feel sleep deprived and how has that has affected your performance? Do you find your classroom performance affected after eating certain foods?
3. Do you feel that you make enough time for your loved ones? If you don't, what particular aspects of the job hold you back? Is there any way that you can rearrange some things in your life so that you can create more time?

Practical Tips

- As much as we love to work (or not), we must try to make sure that we are not sacrificing other parts of our lives for our careers. Don't wait until your health suffers before you make the relevant changes. One of the techniques that I use is what I called my "Rest and Relaxation Schedule." When I was the NEETs coordinator, I would look at my calendar, arrange all my essential meetings and work-related tasks on there and work everything around that, missing lunches and sometimes time with my loved ones. I knew that was unsustainable. So, I tried to flip it around. Using my RnR schedule, I will put all the things that help me relax and recuperate like time with my friends and family, time to exercise or just time with myself and then schedule all my work commitments around that for the week. You must also have what I call 'non-negotiables' in your schedule — things that you have put in your RnR schedule that you will not break under any circumstances. My non-negotiable is that I have dinner with my wife and child every day — that means no marking, no planning, no emails or anything work related. It's family time. It hasn't always been easy, and I have had to make a lot of compromises, but my life overall has been a lot better since I made the change. I know you may not have a lot of time, but try to take some time out for the things you care about. It helps.

- Practice sleep hygiene — these are a set of practices that will help you have a longer and better quality of sleep. I wasn't a believer at first, but after I implemented it, I can honestly say it's really had a positive impact on my life. I've already made some sleep hygiene suggestions in this chapter but I was giving you the basics. Other tips include making sure that your sleeping environment is comfortable, seeing enough natural sunlight and limiting stimulants like caffeine and alcohol especially before bedtime. For the lowdown on how to get better sleep, there are loads of great resources out there. Check out "The National Sleep Foundation" online who have an absolute wealth of materials that will help you get more kip or surf the internet — there is always something that can help you sleep better.

- You don't have to exercise for ten hours to get its benefits. Walking has been a real game-changer for me to help me handle my stress and relax during the day, but there are lots of other things that you can do. I am a big fan of High-Intensity Interval Training (HIIT) which can be done over a five to ten-minute period. If done correctly, it can really help you burn those calories and release those feel-good chemicals. But as always, seek advice before taking on any new exercises. If you are unsure, consult your GP - if you have a heart attack, please do not blame me.

THE UGLY

How To Handle a Flashpoint

Now, let's get ready to rumble. In this chapter, I am going to talk about when you have a full-blown crisis occurring in the middle of your lesson. These are what I call 'flashpoint' situations. A flashpoint in an extremely disruptive situation that stops all learning in the classroom and must be dealt with immediately. If no action is taken, flashpoints escalate out of control and be a danger to yourself and others. Examples include:

- Physical fighting between students
- A medical emergency — a student collapses in the classroom
- Students verbally abusing or threatening towards others in the classroom
- Students throwing dangerous objects around the room or generally being unsafe — such as kicking the door or throwing chairs

I am sure that you can come up with your own scenarios. Any of the situations above can throw your nervous system for a loop and put you any of 'fear responses' that we spoke about in the previous chapter.

For the scope of this book, I won't be covering what you should do in a medical emergency. My advice is simple: become a First Aider. If you can't do that, make sure you know who the designated first aiders are in your institution.

In the next steps, we will be looking purely at behaviour. Flashpoints can be hard to predict, but here are some steps that you can take before, during and after to help you deal with them more effectively and hopefully stop them from occurring in the future.

Prevention

Not all flashpoint situations are the same. Some just happen instantly, but others are like brewing storms — the same way that on a beautiful day we are wary of the dark clouds on the horizon, there are signs that your students can display that will indicate that a flashpoint may happen. You must stay sensitive to changes in your classroom.

As your students grow to trust you, they will give you information about potential conflicts that are brewing between different individuals.

I learnt this the hard way. I was part of an 'Inclusion Team' in large Outer London secondary school. Our team's role was to help the Senior Leadership monitor, control and resolve any negative behaviour problems that affected the student body. My day-to-day duties included talking to parents about the child's behaviour, booking detentions, running inclusions and investigating incidents.

For our more challenging students, we ran mentorship and reflection sessions to try to prevent future flashpoints and provide strategies to help them successfully thrive in their classes.

One of our regulars who always ended up in our office was a young man who I shall call 'Mark.' Mark was diagnosed as having autism but also had an anxiety disorder. Mark by the age of sixteen, was six foot, three inches and sixteen stone of chiselled muscle — with the attitude too. Mark had the build of a heavyweight boxing champion and, despite the efforts of medication and great pastoral support, his behaviour could still be challenging to deal with. He often refused to follow any instructions given by adults and became aggressive at any perceived slight, real or imagined. Mark tended to be fairly relaxed with the Inclusion Team but was extremely stubborn – often leading to many arguments with other members of staff. In general, teachers and students would leave Mark to own devices. Apart from one student – Charlie.

Charlie, who was also in Year 11, was a short, wiry boy — almost the polar opposite of Mark, and wasn't as accommodating as other members of the school community. Whereas other students may have ignored Mark's specific behaviour patterns, Charlie always rose to the occasion, insulting, laughing and belittling him and described it as 'banter.' Mark had started calling Charlie his 'archenemy' and there were rumours that they now had staring matches in the playground. We spoke to the boys individually, and they both assured us that it wasn't a problem and we left it at that.

This all changed when on a lazy Thursday afternoon. I was sitting

THE UGLY

in our office when I heard an almighty crash and howls down the corridor. I quickly ran outside and saw some Year 11 girls running out the classroom screaming. I sprinted into the room, to find that two teachers were trying to stop Mark from trying to beat up Charlie who was at the other end of the room shouting hysterically. Tables were flipped and chairs were strewn all over the classroom. With the help of the other teachers, we managed to guide Mark into our office and try to talk him down. Mark completely lost it and it took three staff members and the Deputy Headteacher to talk him out of doing anything foolish.

After investigating the incident, it was worse than we feared: despite both students saying that the 'beef was squashed,' the bad feelings between the two young men festered and became violent. A concealed weapon was found in Mark's bag. One of the teachers injured their shoulder in the commotion. The police had to be called and a criminal investigation had to be conducted.

As teachers, I know that we have a million things to do. But if you see a recurring negative pattern between your students, don't ignore it.

How you can combat this is by using SIT. See, Investigate and Take action

- **S**ee - Notice anything that is weird or out of place, even if you may think it's nothing.
- **I**nvestigate - If you do notice something strange, don't be scared to ask questions. If there is a conflict stirring, try to find out the cause and see it can be averted. Talk to your Team.
- **T**ake action - If it's dire, report it via the right channels and follow up to see whether it has been resolved.

A quick chat, extra pastoral support or a restorative meeting can save you a whole lot of issues later.

Quarantine

Prevention is not always possible — what if a flashpoint blows up in front of you? Then it is simple: you need to quarantine the situation.

If you have two students kick off in your class, stop the fight and make sure that they are not in the same room until the situation is fully assessed. The separation allows the students to recover from the emotional hijacking and stops further disruptions in your class.

In fire prevention training, you are taught that fire needs three elements to burn; heat, oxygen and fuel — take out one of those elements, then you have no fire. What I have found over the years is that some severe Disrupters (if they are the cause of the situation) tend to get 'amped up' by having an audience and will showboat in front of their mates. This can serve as their 'oxygen.'

State your instructions in a firm but non-emotional manner as possible. If you work yourself up into a state, you will start 'firefighting' which will reduce your authority and make the situation worse. If the student does not comply, state your request again. If by the third time they are still not listening, or they are ramping up the hostility, then call for assistance.

If the students are knocking great lumps out of each other, then please use common sense and call for help. Your institution should have a procedure in which you can send an "SOS" call for someone to come to your aid. There is no shame in asking for help. The faster you quarantine, the quicker you can get the class back into order.

Solve and Sanction

I've put this part at Stage Three, but this can easily be Stage Four. Depending on the situation at hand, you may give a sanction on the spot if the reason is clear cut. But not all flashpoints are the same, and some may require a bit more investigation. Let's go back to our example with Mark and Charlie. Although that flashpoint erupted in that particular classroom, we had to gather statements, talk to witnesses, talk to the police and the parents — this would not have been possible during the lesson. At some point, there must be a resolution. This could involve a writing a formal report, a visit to the Headteacher or a sanction being given.

If you are conducting an investigation, make sure it's as thorough as possible so that you can get the most accurate resolution. Don't sweep anything under the carpet. In my experience, if incidents are not dealt with effectively, like smouldering embers that reignite the fire after being exposed to air, flashpoints can explode again and sometimes get worse. If it is serious, make sure you get your Team involved.

Settle

After you have quarantined the situation, your job is to get your class settled as fast as possible. A major disruption may supercharge everyone's nervous system, and it may take a while for everyone to calm down.

Do not underestimate the time it takes for everyone to regroup. Research has shown those office workers who are interrupted in the middle of a project take "an average of 23 minutes and 15 seconds to get back to the task[8]." How much more would it be for students? Shutdown all conversations about what has happened and set a task that they can preferably work independently on.

From my experience, Compliants and other Disrupters in the class, may try to use the mayhem to their advantage and, like any good D-List Celebrity, try to get their own fifteen minutes of fame. In the aftermath, it's good to be calm but firm in restoring the balance. I know that this is easier said than done, especially if you are in a heightened state. But remember you are the leader and the group takes their cues from you. If a student desperately wants to talk to you, then do that either outside the classroom or ask them to do it after the lesson — your priority is to restore law and order.

Reflection Questions

1. Have you recently had to deal with a flashpoint? Exactly what happened before the flashpoint took place? Where you aware of the signs and could it have been prevented?
2. During the flashpoint, how effective were you at quarantining the incident? Did you ask for help and how did that change the situation? If you weren't successful, why was that and what could you have done to improve?
3. How effective are you at settling the class after an incident?

Have you found that other students try to take advantage of the disruption? What strategies have you used to restore order?

Practical Tips

- Although you may not be able to prevent all flashpoints, certain classes and certain individuals may either cause or be a factor that helps create these situations. If you have a challenging class where flashpoints occur more often, look at your seating plan and reflect upon the dynamics of the room. Who doesn't get on with whom? Who likes to irritate others? Who distracts people around them? Separate certain characters or change certain parts of your lesson plan to minimise the disruption. Get to know your class and use that information to inform your decisions.
- Flashpoints can be seasonal as well. In my experience, a week or two before any major breaks such as Christmas, Easter or the summer holidays tended to have more flashpoints than others. Everyone, including the teachers, gets more fatigued, and behaviour starts to slip. As a result, your teaching windows tend to shorten naturally (see Chapter "Use your Windows Effectively"). Factor this into your lessons towards the end of the term and try to do some activities that are less demanding.
- If flashpoints emotionally distress you and make you feel physically or emotionally unwell, then you will need help. If your classes are a danger to your wellbeing, then this is not OK. This is not good for anyone. It may be that your groups are unbalanced with too many Disrupters or Compliants. This is where your Team becomes vital to help you look at ways of dealing with your students. Don't go it alone.

THE UGLY

Use LAST

In your career, you will face situations where you will have to act more like a guide than a teacher. Life happens. Your students will present you with personal issues that range from tiny irritations to life-changing disasters that have long-term consequences.

If you do not have a way to help your students handle these difficulties, you could easily find yourself overwhelmed and burnt out. The LAST framework was a method that I learnt as an account manager and it was designed to help disgruntled customers, especially those who were going to take their services from our company.

This method is incredibly useful if you find yourself dealing with a student who is distressed or having outside issues that may be a barrier to their learning. This technique can help you take a step back and come up with concrete action plans that can help resolve the problem and emotionally support your student.

Before I introduce you to the framework, I have a few words of caution. You must always maintain the Teaching Standards and Safeguarding procedures that are stipulated by the Government and your institution. If you do encounter extreme or harrowing problems that are not in your capacity to solve, please follow your Safeguarding procedures and get help — but I will discuss that later.

Secondly, NEVER promise to keep secrets or not to disclose vital information. This is part of the Safeguarding procedure in any case, but I have heard of teachers that have broken these rules, and it has had dire consequences for their career. From the outset, always warn your students that, for legal reasons, you may have to pass their information to the relevant authorities, especially if it concerns their wellbeing.

The LAST Framework

L is for Listen

When I was in sales, I was taught that most people don't listen to others. Most of us have 'filters' where we get the information that we feel is important or of interest to us. We listen to interrupt but not to understand. But listening is an absolutely critical skill if you want to be able to get a handle on the difficult situation at hand.

You must learn to listen with the compassion of a mentor but with the logic of a scientist. Dr Stephen Covey described this as 'empathetic listening.' Covey stated that you must "listen with your eyes and your heart. You listen with feeling, for meaning. You listen for behaviour. You use your right brain as well as your left. You sense, you intuit, you feel[9]." Here are a couple of things you should be thinking about when you are listening.

What Is the Core of the Problem?

Sometimes there will be an incident where a student may react to something explosively that wouldn't cause them an issue on a typical day. Imagine one of your best-behaved students screaming at their friend over dropping their pencil then storming out of your classroom. Your job in this particular case is to play detective and try to understand what is triggering this new behaviour.

As I mentioned in an earlier chapter, we all tend to judge and place labels on people. But if you deal with a student regularly and they are presenting negative behaviours, always think of the root of the problem. Look beyond the actions that they display and see if there could have been something that happened outside the classroom. Ask them how their day has been and how they are getting on with their work. A little compassion and intelligence can go a long way.

What Emotional State Are They in?

This is absolutely critical especially if we have students that have SEMH. If, for example, they have just come out of having a major punch-up with another student, the last thing that they would want would be having a teacher bombarding them with questions about their 'feelings.'

In the chapter "How To Handle a Flashpoint" I spoke about being emotionally hijacked and how that was akin to being on a drug. Just listening instead of reacting gives you time to settle and centre yourself, and it will give that individual time to allow these stress responses to work through their system.

If we had a raging customer on the phone, as salespeople, we were trained to stay cool, calm and collected and listen to the customer, no matter what. As long as you didn't aggravate the client and remained polite and professional, most customers would start to calm down as they vented their frustrations. Empathetic listening has this power. As a rule of thumb, the more distressed or angry they are, the more that you will need to listen and not interject until they calm down.

Who Needs to Be in the Loop?

At this stage, for Safeguarding purposes, it is absolutely critical, you pinpoint how severe the issue is and who may need to be involved. Your institution should, as part of its Safeguarding policy, have information on who the designated ports of call are and how they can be reached. For your own professional wellbeing and that of the students, please make sure that you know these processes, and if the issue is severe, that you follow them as your institution dictates. If the situation is dire, then you may need to pass on the details straight away to the relevant people.

Do Not Probe

If you are faced with a delicate situation, remember you are not the police. From a safeguarding standpoint, we are not allowed to 'force' an answer from of our students — they have to disclose that information willingly, without any pressure. It is also not our place to demand answers or to get to the bottom of the issue.

Be a listening ear, but always be mindful that this could be an issue that you may not have the expertise nor the capacity to solve. Ask open-ended, non-threatening questions and give the student enough time and space to answer them, even when you feel that there are uncomfortable pauses. As teachers, sometimes we feel that we must be all things to all people, but that's impossible. If it is a sensitive issue, jump straight the "Send" part of the framework.

A stands for Apologise or Acknowledge

In sales, we were taught that to acknowledge the problem is halfway to solving it. Even if the problem or crisis is nothing to do with you, accept what they have said and, where appropriate, apologise for what they are going through. Human-beings crave affirmation, and the fastest way to build rapport with someone is understand and sympathise with their experience. At appropriate points in the conversation, repeat the main points of what the other person had said previously. This shows that you are listening and you are digesting what you have been told.

If you have done the first two parts - listening to their concerns and acknowledging their experiences, you may find they start to recognise *your* feelings and willing to listen to your suggestions. They may say "sorry sir/miss, it's not you that made me mad" or "I know that I snapped earlier, it's just things are difficult." You have reached a critical part of the conversation — you have now moved from being in a crisis mode to having a dialogue. Other signs could be that seem more comfortable and less agitated by your presence. If this happens, then you are ready to start looking at solutions.

S stands for Solve or Send

This is where you get to the business end of the conversation, where you must put some action steps together. But, as always, there are many landmines you must avoid.

In sales, you are taught that, while you cannot always provide a solution, you can give a resolution. In simple terms, your student may not get exactly what they want, but our job is to find a suitable alternative or try to use this moment as an opportunity for both the student and the teacher to learn how to avoid this situation again.

For example, when I sold high-end furniture, most of what we provided was custom-made, and we told our customer that they had a seven day cool off period. Once those seven days had passed, and we placed the order on our electronic system, we could not refund their money, as we had already paid the manufacturer. No matter how many times I went through this spiel before, during and after the order, there would always be one customer who would want to change their mind. Many of my customer service calls involved telling them that although they couldn't get their money back, they could select another piece of furniture for the same price.

Likewise, if there is a serious incident, this may involve a sanction that cannot be avoided despite the reasoning behind it. There may have to be interventions that at first, may not seem too appealing and your student may resist. But I always remind my students that sometimes these situations are like going to the dentist: unless you are slightly masochistic, we all hate sitting in that chair, surrounded by big needles, loads of drills, and excess charges at the end. But generally, they help us deal with any problems with our teeth that will become major issues later on. The longer you leave things, the worse the situation becomes.

Some issues are part of a more significant problem that may take more than you to solve. This can usually be the case with SEMH students and that's OK - hence why this can sometimes become "Send." Some problems may not be solved overnight and may need some additional help but what is important is that there should be some concrete, definitive steps put in place which will help the student and you can discuss ways that you can help alleviate the problems. In the Chapter, "Assemble Your Team" you can find more details.

If you have a case where you can solve the issue, that's fantastic! Rather than just dictate the solution to your student, try to come up with three options together and walk them through the best solution. Your aim with this process is to teach them to learn how to make better decisions on their own. This will help them avoid these situations in the future.

T stands for Thank

If you have completed the first three parts successfully, you will have to come to a better place than where you first started. The last step is a nice way to end the communication. It also acknowledges what has occurred between the two of you and helps to foster trust and goodwill. In our day-to-day lives, the negative responses we get from people outnumber the positive ones. When we bump into people, they are more likely to swear at us than apologise (especially in London). We were taught that for some customers, our 'thank you' might be the only one that they would hear throughout the day. A 'thank you' displays common courtesy and teaches your student to do the same.

Reflection Questions

- Have you have ever faced a situation with a student that required you to deal with issues that were more pastoral than academic? How well did that go? What went right and what went wrong?
- Have you dealt with a student whose outside issues repeatedly hinder their performance in the classroom? How did you approach that learner? If their issues were delicate or severe, did you request help from the relevant parties? How was that experience for both you and the student?
- Have you felt overwhelmed by the issues and problems of your students? How do you deal with those feelings? Do you speak to people about your feelings and ask for support? If not, why?

Practical Tips

- I realise that if this happens in the middle of the lesson, you cannot stop everything and spend half an hour with this student. If the issue is serious and you feel it will take longer than five minutes to deal with, it's perfectly fine to say to your student to take a timeout outside or elsewhere. They can go to another room to gather their thoughts and then, you can deal with it properly at a time which convenient for the both of you, perhaps at the end of the lesson. Please make sure that you keep your word and do it at the time that you say—if you go against your word, this can damage the trust that you have built up with the student. If these issues are

THE UGLY

- ongoing, speak to their Form Tutor or Mentor and see if they can help support your student outside of lessons. Get your Team involved.
- Dealing with this side of teaching can be extremely difficult, especially if you are dealing with students that have additional learning needs. Burnout is very real, and we underestimate the emotional cost of the job. In the chapter "Assemble Your Team", I talk about the importance of having a support network. These situations may call for someone to lean on. In my account management job, we were assigned to a "buddy" — who was someone, usually more experienced, who would help you if you had issues or someone that you could talk to after a hard day. If you are new to the profession, you will be assigned a mentor. Do not be afraid to speak to your mentor about any issues that come up. They usually can provide you with advice and tools to help you manage your students. If you do not have a mentor, speak to someone in your department or management. A support system makes a positive difference to your well-being. Also, make sure that you look after yourself and you take part in regular self-care.
- This method can take a different turn if YOU are the student's problem. If the student just doesn't like you for whatever reason, they may go out of their way to disrupt your lesson to show their displeasure. If you are unfortunate enough to find yourself in this situation, then I would advise you to arrange a restorative meeting with yourself, the student and the Head of Year/Subject Leader/Mentor/Form Tutor to try and resolve the problem. The same rules still apply, but having an external person can help give you and the student a fresh perspective on the situation. If this still doesn't work, then you may need to have an intervention. See Chapter "Interventions and Letting Go" for more details.

Sanction Quickly and Restore

Unless you have some kind of personality disorder, sanctions are not enjoyable to give. But just like doing your taxes, taking out the bins and cleaning your dog's little 'gifts' off the floor, it has to be done.

Early in my teaching career, I genuinely had a hard time getting my head around sanctions. When I started, I wanted to be a considerate teacher and have all the students like me. But as I have grown as a professional, I realised that I looked at sanctions entirely in the wrong way. Sanctions should be used to discipline and not to punish. Let's take a closer look at these words.

The Oxford Dictionary[10] describes 'punishment' as

1. The infliction or imposition of a penalty as retribution for an offence.

'crime demands just punishment'

Retribution as in revenge. The word punishment comes from the Latin word 'punire' which means 'penalty.'

Fine. Let's look at the word discipline[11]. Several definitions are quite interesting

The controlled behaviour resulting from training.

'he was able to maintain discipline among his men'

1.2 Activity that provides mental or physical training.

'the tariqa offered spiritual discipline'

'Kung fu is a discipline open to old and young'

1.3 count noun A system of rules of conduct.

'he doesn't have to submit to normal disciplines'

The word discipline comes from the Latin word 'discipulus' which means 'learner.' This root word is also where we get the word 'disciple' from.

Although it is subtle, these differences change the paradigm.

THE UGLY

When we sanction our students, it should not come from a place of malice or revenge but from a place of control and justice and should be used to educate and guide our students to follow better patterns of behaviour — patterns that eventually have to follow in the real world.

In wider society, we all have to adhere to laws, regulations and codes of conduct. For good or ill, we as teachers have a responsibility to help prepare our students for the many challenges that they face in the big bad world. Teaching discipline is very much tied into grit and mastery (see the earlier chapter) and many scientific studies have shown that those who can control their impulses and maintain their focus tended to have more successful life outcomes.

The aim of giving sanctions is not to destroy but to build. If done correctly, a sanction should address the misdeed, allow the learner to reflect on their actions and grow a stronger relationship with you in the classroom. Let's look at the steps.

1) Be Careful of the 'Emotional Hijack'

Here's a typical example. Vicky in 1OG is being defiant and will not put her phone away. You have warned her several times and she has now chosen to ignore you.

Your breath is getting shallower, and you start hearing your heartbeat in your ears - you have had to stop the whole lesson and don't understand why Vicky is being this rude. Now you are approaching the danger point. You want to give a sanction, but you are enraged. If you start shouting, Vicky will see the sanction as an act of open aggression and will respond in kind. The situation is heating up. Follow these steps.

- Stay calm — do not lose your cool as it takes away from your authority. Reiterate for the last time what you have asked the student to do and what will be the consequences. At this point you may want to use the 'Easy Road Hard Road' Technique.
- If the student does not comply or ramps up the aggression, then this is where separation must occur to stop the hijack situation. Ask the student to step outside the classroom to

have a breather, or call for additional support. This will give you and the student time to settle your nervous systems, flush out all the stress hormones and hopefully get back to thinking clearly. Unless it is dire, I would suggest holding back from giving a final sanction straight away. Give yourself the space to act with dignity and clarity. Work to deescalate the situation and speak when you are calm and centred.

2) State and Explain the Sanction

Vicky refused to hand her phone over and refused to leave the class, forcing another teacher to come in to assist in removing her from the room. You have arranged a meeting after school to discuss what happened.

There are two ways that you can conduct this meeting. You can step into the class with all guns blazing and, within a minute, lay down the law, make a couple of threats like Vin Diesel and then dismiss the student. But this could reignite the flashpoint and be counterproductive in the long term.

Another way you could do this is by walking them through the chain of events and explaining why that sanction had to be given. Here, you walk through the process, asking the student how they felt and what other decisions they could have made at the key points. If the student is in a calmer state, you could ask her a series of questions that are designed to make her think about her behaviour, and this could be done in under five minutes. Here are some examples:

- Tell me about what you think happened.
- When I asked you to hand over your phone, why did you not do it? How were you feeling at this point?
- Do you feel that was the right response? If it happened again would you make a different choice?

Rather than damning the student, you are encouraging them to reflect and learn from this experience. In the example above, you may find out Vicky had a fight with her Mum in the morning and was texting her Dad to intervene. Vicky may tell you that she is having problems in school with her friends and was texting her sister for support. Although her response was not appropriate, your conversations will give you greater insights into your student's personality, triggers and will provide you with more tools to stop this happening in the future.

Having a dialogue doesn't mean that sanction may necessarily be avoided. At this point, the student may even feel remorse about the incident that occurred. This leads to the third step.

3) Build On the Relationship After the Sanction Has Been Served

If this part was handled correctly, this can be a real opportunity to climb higher with the student up Trust Mountain. Even the infamous political author Niccolo Machiavelli who coined the phrase "it is better to be feared than loved" stated that being a tyrant is not all that is cracked up to be. Machiavelli also wrote, "proceeding to the other qualities mentioned above, I say that every prince must desire to be merciful and not cruel[12]."

You must make your student understand that once their sanction is served, it's a new beginning. It's in the past. If the issue is serious then you may have to have a formal restorative meeting. If it is a minor incident, try to have a two-minute conversation before they enter the classroom. Be positive and show some goodwill. Be willing to try again and ask your student to do the same.

Many of the breakthroughs with my disruptive students came by working out our differences after a sanction was served. Use this as a chance to get to know your student better and if it helps, bring a member of your Team for support - which I will talk about in the next chapter.

Reflection Questions

1. In general, are you a person that hands out sanctions very quickly or do you tend to ignore certain behaviours and sanction later? Why is that? Have your methods been effective and why?
2. Are there certain classes where you feel that you are giving

out more sanctions than others? What reasons can you think of? Have you tried to change these factors and if so what happened?
3. When you give sanctions in general, how are you feeling? Do you give sanctions away in the heat of the moment or do you tend to allow the situation calm down before you give them to the student? In general, how do your students react when you give these sanctions to them?

Practical Tips

- Practice the "Sundown Rule" — where possible, your student should serve the sanction by the close of play that day. Of course, if the issue is serious, this may take a little longer. Make sure that sanctions do not drag on for longer they need to as this creates uncertainty, tension and risks destabilising your relationship with that student. If you regularly find yourself in a situation where sanctions take too long to action, it may be worth talking to your Line Manager or someone senior to smooth out the whole process.
- Be firm but don't be completely rigid. If a student feels really hard done by, give them an opportunity to voice their grievances. Even we make mistakes – have an open dialogue and be willing to listen. Don't create unnecessary animosity. Always use caution and proceed carefully. If they can communicate with you in a calm and measured way, then welcome the conversation. If they are rude or dismissive, then postpone the conversation until they are calmer and they are willing to have a dialogue. If this is a repeated pattern, then get your Team involved and arrange a restorative meeting. Use the gathering as a chance to create a new understanding and iron out any grievances that have happened in class.
- This doesn't always go to plan. A student may ultimately refuse to meet with you or follow any of your sanctions. Do not let this go as this undermines your authority. Actions

THE UGLY

must have consequences. Serial refusers will need stronger interventions. Escalate this up to your Line Manager and speak to their caregivers. Do not struggle in silence as ultimately this will create bigger flashpoints down the line.

Assemble Your Team

Marvel's *The Avengers* was my boyhood dream come true. Although cinematic universes are now widespread these days, in 2012, they were rare and never done to that scale before. I still feel the chills up my spine when I see the Hulk tag-teaming with Thor! Nick Fury played by Samuel L. Jackson assembled the superhero team to fight the threats that no single superhero could face on their own. You must channel your inner Sam Jackson and find some remarkable people to help you on your teaching journey.

No person is an island. Teaching is a team sport. For those who are early in their career, you may feel that you have to do it all on your own. But if you want to be able to last in our profession, you will need to know how, when and who to ask for assistance.

Each institution will be different but here are some suggestions for the types of people you should put in your squad.

Learning Support

These remarkable people will often come into your class and will give focused support to any students that have particular Special Educational Needs (SEN). These students may have an Education, Health and Care Plan (EHC) which will detail their needs extensively. This will take different shapes in different institutions. Teaching Assistants (TAs) usually have an absolute wealth of experience in dealing with SEN and SEMH learners and will help you with the other learners too.

They are the first members of your Team that must befriend. Especially when you are dealing with students who have learning difficulties, TAs can help you identify their routines, learning requirements and triggers which could be the difference between having a good lesson and being in the middle of a flashpoint. Their department is usually run by the Special Educational Needs Coordinator (SENCO). Their departments have a wealth of resources that can provide you with to support your learners.

Another benefit of having these wonderful specialists in your classroom is that they are an extra pair of eyes and ears, helping you identify negative patterns of behaviour and providing valuable insights that you may miss. They can let you know if other students are struggling with your material and what changes you can make to aid them.

Tutors/Mentors

Depending upon your institution, this can come in different flavours. In secondary schools, they often have form tutors who will register and provide pastoral support throughout the academic year. They can give advice, help with sanctions or contact their parents on your behalf. Mentors usually are older students, external agencies or people and they will come in at agreed intervals to offer advice and support that particular learner.

All mentorships are not necessarily academic and can be connected to extracurricular activities. I have worked in schools that have run a whole range of clubs such as football, boxing, chess and even meditation and mindfulness. These activities teach valuable life skills like good communication, discipline, better self-regulation and team working..

Mentors have an extra advantage because they are 'outside' of the normal stream of education and the different setting may help the learner to feel more comfortable and able to express their own individuality.

Head of Departments/Head of Year

These two functions are different: the Head of Department looks after the academic standards of their subject and will work with Senior Management to ensure that factors that such as lesson planning, delivery and marking meet the institution's standards.

The Head of Year will look after the pastoral needs of that particular group of students and will work with the form tutors to track their behaviour and achievements. The Heads of Year also work closely with outside agencies such as the Child and Adolescent Mental Health Services (CAMHS) who can provide specialist support for particular learners. Their job is to help you to look at for the wellbeing of the students in your institution.

From my experience, although both roles are different, these guys will be the people that you will see if the situation is too big to handle on your own. They can help you adjust your lessons to cater for students who do struggle academically or help stage interventions for students how are very disruptive. students. They are immensely experienced and an absolute must-have in your corner.

Counsellors/Therapists

As stated earlier in the book, real life happens. Some of your students may have been affected by extremely traumatic events from their past or may have ongoing issues. Whatever the reasons, these emotional needs may show up in the classroom.

These challenges may manifest themselves in many different ways: extremely challenging behaviour, hyperactivity, hatred of authority or constant daydreaming. These students may have to see a professional counsellor. Counsellors will often give your students tools that will help them cope with their traumas and will work with them to manage any difficult feelings as they arise.

Depending on the nature of their trauma and how sensitive the information is, the counsellor may not be able to disclose the exact nature of your student's challenges. But counsellors can help define the condition that they suffer with and support you in and outside the classroom. They may give you an action plan on how to engage the learner and different approaches if the learner is struggling in your class.

Police/Youth Offending Team

Occasionally, you have a student who has ended up in the Criminal Justice System. If the student has been cleared but is at risk of reoffending or dropping out of education, you may find that you may have to work with the Police and the Youth Offending Services.

Depending on how serious the situation is, your students may have to be placed on 'probation'. In this circumstance, the courts will delay their sentence and young person will be asked to participate in projects like community service or youth crime prevention programmes. If your student reoffends during this time, they will receive a harsher punishment, often going to Youth Offenders institutions.

Some students may have never committed any crimes but may be labelled 'vulnerable.' These students are at risk of becoming involved in anti-social behaviour. Factors could include the area that they live in, family or known associates and prior educational history. If this is the case, the Youth Offending Team (YOT) may get involved, providing workshops and counselling services and will work closely with the educational institution to prevent a negative outcome for the learner's life chances.

Your student may be assigned a police liaison or a key-worker who will help offer support and guidance on what the student's next decisions should be. YOT may work with your student's family as well looking at ways everyone can work together to ensure that the student stays on the straight and narrow.

This list is not absolute. Your institutions may offer different provisions that I may not have even heard of, but the key is knowing what help is there and how to use it.

Here are some quick tips on how to assemble your Team.

1) Network, network, network

I once heard a wise man say that "you should make friends before you need them." This counts more if you are new to your institution.

Learn the lay of the land in your school or college. Find out who is in charge of Behaviour, who are the Heads of the different departments and year groups, who is the SENCO and who are members of Learning Support. Believe it or not, I am an introvert, but I make a point of getting to know as many staff across the institution as possible.

Most teachers that I have ever encountered have been very friendly and have given me great tips on how to handle individual students. This network will be your extra eyes and ears and trust me – you will need them.

2) Have a 'Sit-down'

Like the old Mafia movies, if a student is causing you grief, try to see if you have a 'sit-down' with a couple of members of your Team. Ask if you can have a quick meeting to share ideas and look at behaviour strategies that have worked previously.

I was once a supply teacher in a secondary school and I dealt with a Year 8 student (who I will call Stephen) who had severe emotional dysregulation problems and often had very dramatic outbursts in the classroom. This was a school-wide problem, and the young man felt that all the teachers were picking on him.

The Head of Year 8 called all his regular teachers to come to a meeting with him and his mum after school so that Stephen could communicate his struggles and express what he needed to stay engaged in lessons. In that session, we came up with strategies and fall-back plans if Stephen was having a bad day. Stephen's relationships with all his teachers dramatically improved and the flashpoints halved as a result of this intervention. This is the power of the sit-down.

3) Teach as a Village

After I left the telecommunications industry, I did a stint as 'day supply teacher' to get some experience of school life and keep some money in my pocket. I was absolutely hopeless at first. Classroom room riots happened every lesson, and there was very little I could do about it. As soon as the students heard they were getting a 'supply teacher,' they would become feral, and all I could do was smile in embarrassment. Apart from an SOS email system (that never worked), there wasn't really anyone that I could ask for help. Because I was only there for the day, they correctly guessed that unless they shot me with a crossbow, no further action would be taken. I quickly realised that I had to build up relationships with teachers fast; otherwise I would have been chased out of the school. You can't do it alone – your students need to see your backup.

As you grow closer with your team, your students will realise that their behaviour will have a real impact across the school. Their actions in one lesson now has a direct effect on the others – this can

THE UGLY

be a powerful deterrent for future disruptions. You can also work out rewards, and if you have to, sanctions with the other teachers depending upon their behaviour and make it known that you are communicating with your colleagues.

If you are successful, issues should no longer be slipping through the cracks and every disruption gets followed up. The Compliants and Disrupters will become hesitant to disturb your lessons because they will have five different teachers on their case.

You and your Team are now 'teaching as a village', and this is one of the most effective ways to positively change your disruptive students. But it's not all bad. Make sure that any positive behaviour gets filtered through your network so that they can be encouraged to keep up their great efforts throughout the institution.

In one school I was in, I build a very solid relationship with a PE teacher who was also in charge of the Football Team. One particular student was raising hell in my sessions and was being thrown out of my classes, despite my best efforts. I thought it was hopeless. In frustration, I had a word with the PE teacher and he kicked him off the team and would only reinstate him until his behaviour improved in my classes. That learner became a model student and didn't give me any further problems that year — because we made him an offer he couldn't refuse.

Reflection Questions

1. Do you often communicate with teachers outside of your department? If not, why? What things can you do to change this?
2. If you have a problem with a particular student, who do you go to for help? Is it one person or are there several? How often do you communicate with these people?
3. Do you know who is in charge of Behaviour in your institution? Do you speak to them? Are there extra-curricular activities that your institution provides to help manage behaviour? Do you know how to access them and who would be the right person to speak to?

Practical Tips

- Build a relationship with the teaching assistants that visit your classroom. As a former TA myself, I can honestly say that most go above and beyond the call of duty to help you in your class. Ask them for their advice and absorb all the wisdom that they can offer you. They are indispensable and treat them that way. These are the guys that are in the trenches with you every day and can probably be your main Team members.
- I realise that in your busy day, you may not have thirty minutes to sit-down with other teachers to talk about your students. But I am sure that you find ten minutes in your week to build up your network. Go to lunch with different staff members and don't be shy to ask for advice. Make sure that when the time comes, you do the same thing for them. Besides making new friends, it will pay off when it comes to your birthday — think about that.
- If you do have regular communication with representatives of any external agencies such as CAMHS or the YOT, get to know them and if they have any training days or workshops, I thoroughly encourage you to go. Much of what I have learnt about behaviour management has come from these sessions. They are an absolute goldmine of information and this will give you an edge in your classrooms.

THE UGLY

Get The Carers Onside

In your entire school career, did you ever get a negative phone-call home after one of your 'adventures?' Yes or no?

If you answered 'no' then you are a liar.

Carer contact is never fun for any of the parties involved. When speaking to carers, teachers are required to have an incredible amount of tact, emotional intelligence and empathy to make a successful call. Carers come with their own experiences and viewpoints, and as a teacher, you have to navigate these waters carefully.

But here are a couple of guidelines that will help you make these situations easier and hopefully turn them into positive opportunities.

As always, make sure that you are complying with your institution's protocols.

Meet The Parents

Carer contact is a real game changer and can either make or break your relationship with the student. Remember the 'Student Triangle?' The carer is the bastion of the home. If you make adversaries of the carers, then you most certainly have lost the student.

Look for common ground, areas in which you can work together and focus on results. Each household has its own dynamics — so we must approach each situation with tact, courage and an open mind. Don't assume that the carers will automatically see the world the same way that you do. Whether you are calling or meeting the parents, let's look at it in three stages.

1) Before The Call/Meeting

Here's a tip from my account management days: never go into the meeting cold. Make sure you know who the primary contacts are, the particular needs of the student, the latest concerns about their behaviour and what other members of staff were dealing with this individual. You don't have to spend hours to prepare for your meeting with the carers but for Pete's sake do your due diligence - this can be done in five minutes. Many people make the mistake of just jumping on the phone after your student has gone rogue especially if they have been 'emotionally hijacked' — this can be a recipe for disaster. Here are the basics:

- Something to make notes with - Taking notes will help you capture information that will be useful in the future. I have seen teachers communicate with parents for half an hour on the phone and when I have asked them what the key pieces of information were, they forgot them. Note taking helps you recall the info and keeps you engaged on the call.
- The Educational Health Care Plan (EHC) - if you know that your student has been diagnosed with a specific condition, they should have their EHC plan or statement. Take a moment to read it and make sure that you understand the particulars of their condition and the Action Plan to help the student. You don't have to do this every time, but make sure that you are reviewing them every so often. Sometimes they can change and you don't want to be caught flatfooted. Speak to your Team and make sure you have as much info as possible.
- Have an agenda - write out a plan from your phone call/meeting and the key points that you wish to discuss. What annoys parents (and most people) is a meeting that goes around in circles with no end in sight. Go through what you want to discuss and ask politely if there anything they wish to talk about. If it's not on the plan, then don't talk about it.

2) During the Call/Meeting

This is the tricky part. If an incident has taken place, this has already created a challenging atmosphere. No decent carer wants to hear anything negative about their child, and this may automatically put them on the back foot. Take a deep breath and walk through these steps.

THE UGLY

- Be clear, direct and professional - Explain to the carer what has happened or what has been happening and where necessary show the evidence. Clearly explain what rules or policies that the student may have broken. Do not sugarcoat the issue and spell out any potential consequences. While you are relaying this information, be polite, fair and keep to your professional standards during your interaction. Even if you do feel personally offended or affected by what has been going on, you still must speak with authority and dignity. If you make it sound like a personal crusade against the learner, this may alienate the carer even further.

- Emphasise that you are on the same team - Don't pepper the parent with negative after negative about your student. Make it clear that you called to look at ways in which you and the carers can work together to find a way to resolve any particular issues.

- Listen - It's really critical that you take time to listen to what the parents have to say about this situation. In my time, I have seen a vast variety of reactions from anger, despair, indifference, disbelief and sad acceptance. No matter what the circumstances, listen and try to answer their concerns and questions. A carer's response to our communications can be coloured by their own school experiences. If the parents themselves had a hard time in school, they may automatically come in with a negative bias towards you. Our jobs are to build bridges, not confrontations. If the parent is particularly angry or upset, try to stay composed, professional and if necessary be firm on your personal boundaries if they are being particularly rude or aggressive. Play the detective — try to look for any information that can help you get that breakthrough with your student.

- Talk next steps and have an agreed plan - No matter what happens, try to get some concrete steps and try to get a consensus of what to do next. Depending on what the issue is, it can be a referral to a particular service, a behaviour plan, an adjustment in the learning timetable — you get the idea.

What is also important is that you open a channel of communication. If the parents have any queries, they can reach out to you or another member of staff. If the carers know that you are trustworthy and genuinely care about their child, they will be more willing to work closer with you. This often is the key to turning your students around.

3) After the Call/Meeting and Going Forward

Make sure that all the relevant information is stored on the system and all relevant parties are informed. You may need further meetings to establish how to implement the plan that you agreed to. Try to keep the carers in the loop as much as you can – this can help them feel less anxious and can make the whole process go smoother.

Lastly, make sure that you are not only calling parents for negative reasons. If the student has shown improvement and you are climbing higher with them up Trust Mountain, make sure that you give feedback to the carers. A short phone call or email can go miles with improving your relationship with your pupils. In their eyes, you stop being a monster and start being a person that they can have a positive relationship with.

Reflection Questions

1. In general, what have been your experiences when you have called/met carers about their children? Have they been productive or complete wastes of time? What made them so?
2. What strategies have you used in the past to build positive relationships with parents? How much preparation went into these interactions if any? What strategies worked and what didn't?
3. Have you ever interacted with parents who were either emotionally distressed, angry or defensive? What did you do to smooth out the situation? Did you learn any lessons from this experience and if so what were they?

Practical Tips

- There will be times that no talking, understanding and listening will win over the angry or defensive parent. Sadly, there may be parents that are totally defensive and will justify their child's actions. Some parents won't care and will be utterly apathetic to their child's actions. Don't lose heart. If this happens, do not hesitate to get either your Line Manager involved or someone on the Senior Leadership Team. They can help enforce any decisions that have been made and will provide backup.

- Make sure that you set reasonable expectations about how regularly you will be able to communicate with parents. I had once had a particular parent who either tried to contact me every day to find out the progress of her son — although I admired her enthusiasm, I couldn't keep up with her demands and told her politely and professionally that it would be better to decrease our correspondence! We are all busy teachers with lessons to plan, data to enter and pupils to teach and cannot spend the day sitting on the phone. In sales, we had "Service Level Agreements" or SLAs - which was a service promise that we made to our customers within a set amount of parameters. Set your own SLAs - give the parents your "Office Hours" when they can contact you.

- In the "Use LAST" chapter, I provided the LAST framework, which was a sales technique that I learnt to help me handle difficult conversations with customers. Dealing with parents can be interesting at the best of times so have the framework in your back pocket to help make the call/meeting is productive. Go back to that chapter and refresh yourself.

Interventions and Letting Go

One of my favourite films of all time is 1995's *HEAT* directed by Michael Mann. The film revolves around sleek bank robber and criminal mastermind, Neil McCauley played by Robert De Niro and his game of wits with LAPD Detective Vincent Hanna played by Al Pacino. After McCauley's crew commit a vicious bank robbery, Hanna and his team must find McCauley and his gang before they flee the town with the score. With the clock ticking and tensions escalating, both men test each other's skill, determination and wits as McCauley tries to escape with Hanna doggedly in pursuit..

Despite the two of these men being on opposite sides of the law, both men recognised the other's genius and tenacity. Over the course of the film, a grudging respect started to develop between them. They noticed that they had a fair amount in common: both had failing personal lives, both enjoyed their careers, and both realised that they were reaching the end of their peak years. But both men understood that they were not going to stop with their objectives and were prepared to take each other out if they needed to.

Likewise, you may feel that you have a similar relationship with some of your challenging students. You may face an elite level Disrupter who may not dislike you personally but, for whatever reason, will refuse to behave and work with you. No matter how many strategies you try, no matter how many phone calls that you make home, they will still disrupt your lesson.

At this point you will have to decide: do you ignore everything that they do and hope for the best or do you take action? If their behaviour is just intolerable then you will need to have a HEAT conversation - aka an intervention.

I realise that this chapter may not apply to everybody. I wrote this chapter for the people who:

- May have to conduct a formal intervention
- May have to make the decision whether the student stays on the course or is removed

As the NEETs coordinator, I often found myself in the

unenviable position of having to do both these things. This is never an easy task. Many things have to be weighed up. But sometimes you have tried every strategy in the book and none of them seem to be working? What do you do then?

An intervention is more than just a quick 'chat' but a real fork in the road that will determine whether your students continue on the course or is removed. As always, follow your own protocols.

Your aim in intervention to get a deeper understanding of your student and look at practical ways that their behaviour can be changed promptly and significantly. Interventions are a great way to bring in other members of the school community that can perhaps see alternative solutions that you may have missed. Let's take a closer look.

Thank the Student and Find Something Positive to Say About Them

Interventions tend to carry severe consequences and come with inherent tension. If you have called an intervention, you may feel like the world is on your shoulders. Your student may feel under siege like the world is against them. You start as you mean to go on. It's not a verbal beatdown but a robust discussion about how the learner can change course before it is too late. At the beginning of the meeting, always try to find something good to say about your student. I know that this can sometimes be extremely difficult but start with goodwill. Showing that respect and courtesy can help you create enough of a positive vibe that can set the meeting in the right direction.

Be Frank and Let Them Know How Important This Meeting is

From the outset, be open and honest. The stakes are high. At this point in the meeting, you may talk about:

- What the particular issue is
- The previous steps that have taken to try to remedy it — you can talk about what went well and what didn't go so well

- What is the aim of the meeting — usually interventions take place when other strategies have failed. Don't be afraid to let the carers, the student and any other members of the school community know what has been put in place hasn't worked and another solution must be found. Invite discussions on what can be used in the new plan and look at where collectively you all need to adapt and change.

- Assert the boundaries of the institution - If they have had repeated patterns of harmful and disruptive behaviour and there have been no signs of real progress, apply the 'heat' in the conversation. If the student is consistently ignoring and flaunting these conventions, then the aim of the meeting to ask the question whether that student can be a part of that community. This can never be taken lightly — but as I mentioned before when talking about the Social Contract, your responsibility is to ensure that you create a learning environment where everyone can prosper.

- What are the alternative provisions if this doesn't work out — if there is a choice, don't be afraid to talk about the different options that would be available to the student. This doesn't have to be all doom and gloom. If your institution is not the best fit, then this is the time to look at a different place where they will be able to thrive. Maybe they may benefit from having a different teacher, trying another course or perhaps a different method of learning. Be open-minded and put all the options on the table.

Remember, when you reach the end of each stage, always make sure that you are checking in with the student. If the student has their carers or mentors with them, this could be a great time to get their side of the story and see their perspective. Also, allow the students and their representatives to be honest with you. Endeavour to create a safe environment where their views are honoured and respected, and they can speak freely about what they believe can be changed. An excellent technique to use in these situations is LAST – see the relevant chapter for details.

Have An Agreed Plan of Action

THE UGLY

Once you have looked at what needs to be fixed and how it can be done, you need to create a system where their progress can be monitored and evidenced.

When I was NEETs coordinator, we placed our students "on probation" which mean that for a fixed period, we would monitor their behaviour and we would have regular meetings and talk to their other tutors to see how they are progressing. In some secondary schools that I have worked in, they have a written report that is given to each teacher at the end of each session where the teacher will decide whether they have met their individual targets. The method that you choose will be determined by the needs of your student and your organisation.

No matter what method you chose, it is vital that you get some 'buy-in' from the student and all the other people involved. Remind all parties that these measures are to HELP the student to do better rather than get rid of them. I know, it sounds like a Jedi Mind trick but it is true — it's in every person's benefit that the student can work through their challenges and that the organisation provides support. Find a system that you, the caregivers and perhaps the other staff in your institution will be comfortable with. The more that each party agrees to implement your plan, the more likely that you will succeed.

In must institutions that I have worked in, to remove or transfer a student has real costs in terms of money, time and effort. For the student, this can cause additional anxiety and lost learning and for the teachers and admin staff, this can add to their overloaded in-tray to make sure it is done correctly.

Set up the timetable and stick to it. If your student does improve, lavish praise on them and keep encouraging them to continue. If they feel discouraged but is still making improvements, contrast how they were before and where they are now in their journey. This can be the extra incentive for your student to keep on going.

How To Let Go

At some point in your career, you will see one of your students get removed from the institution. You can't save them all. Like the sun rises and sets, this is just the facts of teaching.

You will face situations where there is just nothing that can be done to keep the student in your institution. The reasons can be as numerous as the pages in this book. Maybe you have had far too many interventions and the student may not want to continue.

Maybe the offence that the student had committed was just too dangerous to warrant him or her returning to the school community. Maybe your class wasn't the right fit for them, or the subject that they were learning wasn't the right for their aspirations.

I wish that I could tell you that in my teaching career, I have managed to turn around every single student and nobody fell by the wayside, but that would be completely unrealistic. There have been students that I have genuinely liked but for a whole truckload of reasons, were removed from the class and no longer allowed to continue. Some students were doing incredibly well but made the wrong choice at the wrong time and were excluded. Other students may have done nothing wrong but because of external factors like family member addictions or housing issues, sadly had to leave us.

Sometimes they are too harmful to the school community. The needs of the many must outweigh the needs of the few. Sadly you may meet students who like Heath Ledger's Joker in *The Dark Knight* just want to "see the world burn" — if that is the case, then you don't really have any options.

Sometimes you will have to let them go.

Behaviour never works in a vacuum. No matter what your personal beliefs are, I am sure most of you would not disagree with me when I say that the world we live in can be cruel and unforgiving. Over the years, I have met some remarkable young people who despite their horrific upbringings, managed to overcome their challenges and go on to lead better lives. I believe our institutions should be catalysts of change, and we are their guides, showing them that their stories do not have to end tragically.

THE UGLY

Their disruptive behaviour could be a mask for their pain. However, this should never be an excuse to make anyone else's life a living hell or stopping other people's learning. We are all human and yes, we sometimes want to lash out at the world for what has happened to us. Students sometimes feel like we don't get it, but we do. But if they are not willing to meet us even part of the way, then perhaps it is best to let them find their own path and not impose our ideas upon them.

Regardless of the reason, when that time comes where the student can no longer continue, always try to handle it with grace, understanding and empathy. Where possible and if you are involved, try to help the student and the family find somewhere that may be better for their own unique needs and be sincere in your attempts.

If I ever had to be involved in exiting a student, I always tried to encourage them that although it didn't work out with us, it doesn't mean that it won't work anywhere else. Although they may not see it now, this could be the start of something better. We didn't get into the teaching game to reach this outcome but look at these situations as learning experiences - what you learn there will help another student in the future.

Reflection Questions

1. Have you ever had to either ask for a student to be removed from your class/course/institution? What was the reason? What was the key lesson that you learnt from that experience? What could you do better next time?
2. Do you currently have any students that have just remained Disrupters despite all your efforts? Is this student disruptive the majority of his other classes? What interventions have you put in place for this student? Have they worked?
3. Have you already had formal interventions with this learner and it hasn't worked? What conditions of the Action Plan haven't been met? Have you asked for additional support from the carers and your Team? What alternative provisions have you looked at?

Practical Tips

- For this chapter, I only have one takeaway and it's simple. You must try to do everything that you can to try to avoid getting to this point. If you do have a Disrupter and they have displayed the same behaviour over many classes, this should be flagged up straight away and the student should be receiving additional help. If this is the case, your Team should be heavily involved and you must work together to secure the best outcome. Go through all the techniques in the "Ugly" section and make them a part of your behaviour tool kit. This situation is not comfortable, but it is survivable — hang in there.

Epilogue

Become The Hero Of Your Own Film

We Started From The Bottom and Now We are Here

On that cold May day in 2014, I remember standing with my group of young students at the bottom of this gigantic, beautiful building in complete awe. I was wearing my fancy brown, bespoke tailored suit, (the one I usually wear for weddings that I care about) and I still felt underdressed. My students were… well, unimpressed. We told them to dress smartly for the occasion, and some of them just wore their best black Nike Air Maxes. One lad even managed to wear a blazer — well, that was a massive achievement for him at least. We pushed past the surprisingly heavy glass doors and made our way into the lobby.

After many hard, gruelling months, most of our students had passed their assessments, and most of them had chosen to go into Further Education. When we first got these guys, most of them were kicked out of school, angry and had really bleak life outcomes. Now armed with these qualifications, they had a fighting chance and a clear road for a better future. Our mission was complete and now it was time to celebrate and shake a leg.

One of the funders of our project was a huge multinational bank with multiple offices around the world. As part of their Corporate Responsibility Strategy, they put out a bid to the local colleges in the area to design a project that will help the most at risk, vulnerable young people in East London and give them the skills and tools to access Further Education or decent employment. The bank was so pleased with our results that they invited the students, along with our other partners to their swanky Head Office in the heart of Canary Wharf to hand out their certificates and have a little soiree in their honour. The host was one of the Senior Directors of the bank, and my boss told me that there were going to be a lot of big wigs at this party. This was a big deal.

For my students, this was a waste of time. They just wanted to be back at the Centre making music, shooting films and being creative. One of our boys said, "Bruv I don't have no time to meet some boring old stiffs — ain't they got things to do like, writing spreadsheets or something?" We are laughed and told him to be polite, but that didn't lift his mood. But as we stepped out of the elevator right on the top floor and we were greeted by the beautiful London skyline through the French glass windows, the other teachers and I saw their irritation turn to excitement — now they knew this was no ordinary day.

The waiters brought around all these fancy dishes salmon canopies, posh cheeses and the fancy crackers you see in the films. Our students weren't interested in any of that but went straight for the pizzas and ate to their heart's content. The Director came out and spoke about community, education and why it was essential to invest in the young people of London and the success of the project.

He then asked me to come on stage to make a short speech about the program. I was taken completely off guard. I had nothing prepared. With my mouth half full of salmon and cheese, I hastily made my way to podium asking myself what on Earth am I going to say without my students laughing at me.

But as I stood on the stage and saw the faces of my students, fellow tutors, youth workers and individuals that made our project possible, I realised something.

It was all worth it.

Despite the stress, the downtimes, the ruined lessons, the frustrations and the meetings, we made a difference. A real difference in the lives of our students and, in our tiny way, made our city a better place.

And that is exactly what I said that day.

I felt like an Action Hero - and I hope that in a tiny way, this book will help you feel like that in your classrooms, your institution and your world.

We Can't Stop 'Cos We Won't Stop

Well, we have come to the end. I have given you my theories, tips, tricks and strategies to help you in your classroom. I want to say a massive thank you for hanging with me and getting to the end of this book. I hope that this book has given you new tools and techniques that will make you feel more like the Action Hero of your classroom.

Some of you may think that because I wrote this book, all my classes must run smoothly, and even the most disruptive students fall under my spell. Well, let me burst that bubble right there — it's still hard work and I don't win every battle. Sometimes I don't get the balance right and I have my wobbles. I still have days when I am frustrated, tired, worn out and fed-up — teaching is not a walk in the park. There are some students that no matter how hard I try, I cannot build that relationship and we are stuck at Level One on Trust Mountain.

Early in my career, when I experienced these setbacks, I would automatically beat myself up about it, feeling like a 'failure' and questioning why I ever decided to be a teacher. But through great mentors, training and hard-fought life experience, I have realised that although you may lose some battles, it doesn't mean that you have lost the war.

If you think of your favourite action film, the hero/heroine often has to be put through the wringer perhaps losing their home, their reputation and even their loved ones before they find the strength to overcome their rivals and save the day. Let me put it to you this way, would you go and watch a film where the hero found everything easy and he or she saved the day with ease? Hell no! It would be boring! There are no magic bullets, take a breath and embrace the struggle my friends — if it doesn't kill you, it will only make you better.

I wanted to leave you with something motivational — something that will inspire you when the going gets tough. When looking at quotes, I was thinking of the old classics like Teddy Roosevelt's "Man In The Ring" or Winston Churchill's "We Will Fight On The Beaches" — but that's a bit cliché. But I found a quote from the bestselling author Seth Godin which I think sums up what it takes to be a better teacher. Seth said:

> "The rule is simple: The person who fails the most will win. If I fail more than you do, I will win. Because in order to keep failing, you've got to be good enough to keep playing.

EPILOGUE

> So, if you fail cataclysmically and never play again, you only fail once. But if you are always there shipping, putting your work into the world, creating and starting things, you will learn endless things.
>
> You will learn to see more accurately, you will learn the difference between a good idea and a bad idea and, most of all, you will keep producing[13]."

Go out and try things. Fail and fail again. Fail better. Fail forward.

My final challenge to you is this: make your own rules. My rules are a good start but only YOU can be the hero of your own classroom. You may find things that work for you, that I haven't thought of.

Try to see if you can add at least one of your own strategies to the "The Good," "The Bad" and "The Ugly" sections of this book and keep track of the results that you get. Develop your own style and execute it with flair. As much as I like to teach, I also love to be taught and I would love to hear from you! If you have any suggestions, tips, tricks or feedback, mosey on down to the website www.actionheroteacher.com and go to the "Contact" page.

Thank you for rocking with me and wish you all the good fortune in the world for this career called teaching!

Until next time.

Karl C. Pupe

Acknowledgements

First of all, I thank GOD that I was able to make this book at all.

I want to thank my wife Natalie for being my editor, business partner, sounding board, counsellor and book critic all rolled into one. Thank you for taking care of our daughter while I was screaming in frustration and banging my head on the computer screen while writing this book. I could not have done this without you.

A special thank you goes to all my friends who encouraged me to write the book despite my reservations and fears. It means a lot!

To all the teachers that read the book and gave me constructive feedback and helped me to enhance my writing, I want to thank you for bearing with me.

A very special mention goes to Community Music Ltd, and I want to thank Maricia Klincke, Sam Johnson, Matt Murs, Trevor McKinley and Rich Clegg for either putting me on or helping me with the NEETs Project - thank you for your faith in me. All of the other CM family, thank you so much for everything!

Thank you Lee aka West Ham man! You have helped me so many times with so many different projects that I honestly feel like I owe you one of my children or something… Thank you, legend.

Thank you to all the schools, colleges, universities and teaching agencies that I had the pleasure of working with over the years. Your training has been invaluable.

I want to thank to all my students who encouraged me over the years to write a book. This is the first one but I will write one specifically for you guys — don't worry.

Lastly thank you Isabella - you are Daddy's greatest inspiration. Everything I do is ultimately for you and you make me feel like an Action Hero.

Thank you for reading!

Bibliography

Trust Mountain & The Social Contract

1. Pixabay, (2018), *Grand Teton National Park Mountains* [ONLINE]. Available at: https://pixabay.com/en/grand-teton-national-park-mountains-1728535/

2. Wikipedia, (2002), *Maslow's hierarchy of needs* [ONLINE]. Available at: https://en.wikipedia.org/wiki/Maslow%27s_hierarchy_of_needs#/media/File:MaslowsHierarchyOfNeeds.svg

3. Maslow, A. (1943). *A Theory of Human Motivation*. 1st ed. [ebook] Toronto: Christopher D. Green, p.1. Available at: http://citeseerx.ist.psu.edu/viewdoc/download?doi=10.1.1.318.2317&rep=rep1&type=pdf

4. Oxford Dictionary. 2018. *Definition of authority in English*. [ONLINE] Available at: https://en.oxforddictionaries.com/definition/authority.

5. Maxwell, R., 2007. *The 21 Irrefutable Laws Of Leadership*. 2nd ed. Nashville, Tennesse, USA: Thomas Nelson. Page 21

6. Fox Cabane, O., 2012. *The Charisma Myth: Master the Art of Personal Magnetism*. 1st ed. United States of America: Penguin Group. Page 18

7. Maxwell, R., 2007. *The 21 Irrefutable Laws Of Leadership*. 2nd ed. Nashville, Tennesse, USA: Thomas Nelson. Page 79

8. Goleman, D., 1996. *Emotional Intelligence: Why it Can Matter More Than IQ*. 1st ed. Great Britain: Bloomsbury Publishing PLC. Page 34

9. Cambridge Dictionary. 2018. *Definition of empathy in English*. [ONLINE] Available at: https://dictionary.cambridge.org/dictionary/english/empathy

10. Cambridge Dictionary. 2018. *Social Contract*. [ONLINE] Available at: https://dictionary.cambridge.org/dictionary/english/social-contract.

11. Harry Cockburn. 2018. *The UK's strangest laws that are still enforced*. The Guardian [ONLINE] Available at: https://www.independent.co.uk/news/uk/home-news/uk-strangest-weird-laws-enforced-christopher-sargeant-sturgeon-armour-a7232586.html.

12. Ortiz Crespo, R., 2010. *The Active Listener*. 1st ed. USA: lulu.com Page 13.

The Good

1. Carnegie, D., 2006. *How To Win Friends and Influence People*. 1st ed. United Kingdom: Vermillion. Page 237

2. Carol Dweck. 2016. *'Praise the effort, not the outcome? Think again'*. TES [ONLINE] Available at: https://www.tes.com/news/praise-effort-not-outcome-think-again.

3. Alix O'Neil. 2015. *Edinburgh Fringe: why up-and-coming comedians are making serious bucks*. Evening Standard [ONLINE] Available at: https://www.standard.co.uk/lifestyle/esmagazine/edinburgh-fringe-why-up-and-coming-comedians-are-making-serious-bucks-a2488811.html.

4. Achor, S., 2013. *Before Happiness: Five Actionable Strategies to Create a Positive Path to Success*. 1st ed. United Kingdom: Virgin Books. Page 208

5. Robert Cumber. 2015. *Mo Farah used to be a bad loser, says former PE teacher*. getwestlondon.co.uk [ONLINE] Available at: https://www.getwestlondon.co.uk/news/west-london-news/mo-farah-used-bad-loser-8822578.

6. Cahal Milmo. 2010. *Mo Farah: How Britain's athletics hero escaped the

chaos of Somalia. The Independent [ONLINE] Available at: https://www.independent.co.uk/sport/general/athletics/mo-farah-how-britains-athletics-hero-escaped-the-chaos-of-somalia-2037996.html.

7. Rosenthal, R, Jacobson, L, 1965. Pygmalion in the classroom. *The Urban Review*, [Online]. 1, 20. Available at: https://superchargeyourlife.de/wp-content/uploads/2017/10/Glaubenssaetze_3_Rosenthal_Jacobson.pdf

8. Peter, G., 2011. *Tell To Win: Connect, Persuade, and Triumph with the Hidden Power of Story*. 1st ed. Great Britain: Profile Books Ltd. Page 20

9. Peter, G., 2011. *Tell To Win: Connect, Persuade, and Triumph with the Hidden Power of Story*. 1st ed. Great Britain: Profile Books Ltd. Page 21

10. Oakley, B., 2014. *A Mind For Numbers: How to Excel at Math and Science (Even If You Flunked Algebra)*. 1st ed. United States of America: Penguin Group. Page 75

11. Oxford Dictionary. 2018. *Definition of culture in English*. [ONLINE] Available at: https://en.oxforddictionaries.com/definition/culture.

12. Carnegie, D., 2006. *How To Win Friends and Influence People*. 1st ed. United Kingdom: Vermillion. Page 79

13. Wilson, L., 2014. *Practical Teaching: A Guide to Teaching and Training Sector*. 2nd ed. United Kingdom: Cengage Learning EMEA. Page 38

14. Jake, B., 2004. *Ready to Die: The Story of Biggie Smalls-Notorious B.I.G.: Fast Money, Puff Daddy, Faith and Life After Death*. 1st ed. United States of America: Amber Communications Group, Inc. Page 64

15. Haroon Siddique. 2018. *Mental health referrals in English schools rise sharply*. The Guardian [ONLINE] Available

at: https://www.theguardian.com/society/2018/may/14/mental-health-referrals-in-english-schools-rise-sharply-nspcc.

16. Natasha Devon. 2018. *Transform school culture to boost mental health*. [ONLINE] Available at: https://www.tes.com/news/transform-school-culture-boost-mental-health.

17. Duckworth, A., 2018. *Grit: Why passion and resilience are the secrets to success*. 1st ed. United States of America: Scribner. Page 8

18. Carol, D., 2012. *Mindset: Changing The Way You think To Fulfil Your Potential*. 1st ed. United States of America: Ballantine Books. Page 5

19. Olson, J., 2013. *The Slight Edge: Turning Simple Disciplines Into Massive Success & Happiness*. 8th ed. Austin, Texas USA: Greenleaf Book Group Press. Page 72

20. Kreeft, P., 2018. *Philosophy 101 by Socrates: An Introduction to Philosophy Via Plato's Apology*. 1st ed. United States of America: Ignatius Press. Page 16

The Bad

1. Wikipedia. 2018. *Pareto Principle*. [ONLINE] Available at: https://en.wikipedia.org/wiki/Pareto_principle.

2. Cloud, H. And Townsend, J. 1992. *Boundaries*. 1st ed. United States of America: Zondervan. Page 36

3. Emma Elsworthy. 2017. *Average British attention span is 14 minutes, research finds*. The Independant [ONLINE] Available at: https://www.independent.co.uk/news/uk/home-news/attention-span-average-british-person-tuned-in-concentration-mobile-phone-a8131156.html. [Accessed 31 August 2018].

4. Wikipedia. 2018. *Dunning–Kruger effect*. [ONLINE] Available at: https://en.wikipedia.org/wikiDunning%E2%80%93Kruger_effect.

5. Cialdini, R., 1999. *Influence: Psychology of Persuasion*. 2nd ed. United States of America: William Morrow. Page 57

6. Baumeister, R. & Tierney, J, 2012. *Willpower: Why Self-Control is The Secret to Success*. 1st ed. Great Britain: Penguin. Page 1

7. 25. Oakley, B., 2014. *A Mind For Numbers: How to Excel at Math and Science (Even If You Flunked Algebra)*. 1st ed. United States of America: Penguin Group. Page 103

8. Simon Worrell. 2018. *You Need Your Personal Space—Here's the Science Why*. National Geographic [ONLINE] Available at: https://news.nationalgeographic.com/2018/01/personal-space-between-us-graziano-peripersonal-dyspraxia/.

9. Rachel Gillet. 2016. *11 nervous habits that make you look incompetent*. Business Insider UK [ONLINE] Available at: http://uk.businessinsider.com/nervous-habits-that-make-you-look-incompetent-2016-8?r=US&IR=T/#-1.

10. Vanessa Van Edwards & Brandon Vaughn. 2015. *5 Secrets of a Successful TED Talk*. Scienceofpeople.com [ONLINE] Available at: https://www.scienceofpeople.com/secrets-of-a-successful-ted-talk/.

11. Grabo, Allen & Vugt, Mark. (2016). Charismatic Leadership and the Evolution of Cooperation. Evolution and Human Behavior. 37. 10.1016/j.evolhumbehav.2016.03.005. Page 8

12. BBC. 2017. *Donald Trump's Mexico wall: Who is going to pay for it?*. [ONLINE] Available at: https://www.bbc.co.uk/news/world-us-canada-37243269.

13. Adams, S., 2017. *Win Bigly: Persuasion in a World Where Facts Don't Matter*. 1st ed. New York: Portfolio Penguin.

14. Greene, R., 2000. *The 48 Laws Of Power*. 1st ed. Great Britain: Profile Books Ltd.

The Ugly & Epilogue

1. National Institute for the Clinical Application of Behavioural Medicine. 2017. *How Anger Affects the Brain and Body*. [ONLINE] Available at: https://www.nicabm.com/how-anger-affects-the-brain-and-body-infographic/.

2. James McConchie. 2018. *What Do Teens' Emotions Feel Like?*. Great Good Magazine [ONLINE] Available at: https://greatergood.berkeley.edu/article/item/what_do_teens_emotions_feel_like.

3. Timmins, W., 2008. *The Chronic Stress Crisis How Stress is Destroying Your Health and What You Can Do To Stop It*. 1st ed. Bloomington, IN, United States of America: AuthorHouse. Page 19

4. Faulkner, G. et al 2005. *Exercise, Health and Mental Health: Emerging Relationships*. 1st ed. Oxon, Great Britain: Routledge.

5. Samantha Mathewson. 2017. *Here's What Happens in the Brain When You Don't Get Enough Sleep*. Livescience.com [ONLINE] Available at: https://www.livescience.com/60875-sleep-deprivation-sluggish-brain-cells.html.

6. Ron Friedman. 2014. *What You Eat Affects Your Productivity*. Harvard Business Review [ONLINE] Available at: https://hbr.org/2014/10/what-you-eat-affects-your-productivity.

7. Nicola Davis. 2016. *People with more friends have higher pain thresholds, study suggests*. The Guardian [ONLINE] Available at: https://www.theguardian.com/science/2016/apr/28/people-with-more-friends-have-higher-pain-thresholds-study-suggests.

8. Kermit Pattison. 2018. *Worker, Interrupted: The Cost of Task Switching*. Fast Company [ONLINE] Available at: https://www.fastcompany.com/944128/worker-interrupted-cost-task-switching.

9. Covey, S., 2004. *The 7 Habits of Highly Effective People*. 15th ed. United Kingdom: Simon & Schuster. Page 241

10. Oxford Dictionary. 2018. *Definition of punishment in English*.

EPILOGUE

[ONLINE] Available at: https://en.oxforddictionaries.com/definition/punishment.

11. Oxford Dictionary. 2018. *Definition of discipline*. [ONLINE] Available at: https://en.oxforddictionaries.com/definition/discipline.

12. Machiavelli, N., Bondanella, P. 1998. *The Prince (Oxford World's Classics)*. 1st ed. United States: Oxford University Press. Page 55

13. Sonia Thompson. 2016. *Why Tons of Failure Is the Key to Success, According to Seth Godin*. Inc.com [ONLINE] Available at: https://www.inc.com/sonia-thompson/why-tons-of-failure-is-the-key-to-success-according-to-seth-godin.html.